40 ways to teach in groups

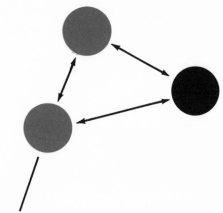

40 ways
to teach
in groups

Martha M. Leypoldt

judson press, valley forge

40 WAYS TO TEACH IN GROUPS

International Standard Book No. 0-8170-0376-2

Library of Congress Catalog Card No. 67-22215

Printed in the U.S.A.

If you think

that the only way to teach

youth or adults

is to lecture to them,

this book is for you.

acknowledgments

THE AUTHOR EXPRESSES APPRECIATION to many persons who assisted in the preparation of the script and who gave helpful comments. Special appreciation is expressed to Roy Seibel, John McKinley, Gertrude Revoir, and the staff members of the Department of Christian Education of the North American Baptist General Conference.

Much of the contents of this book was originally prepared with adults in mind. In time, however, the author and the publishers became convinced that it was equally applicable to the teaching of young people, especially mature senior high students, and it is therefore being published in that form.

M.M.L.

contents

1.

teaching in groups

LEARNING IS A COMPLICATED PROCESS which poses unique difficulties for young people and adults. Teaching them, however, presents a challenge to the adventurous teacher.

The young person or adult approaches a learning situation differently from children, and his processes of learning are different. Before studying specific ways that assist him to learn, however, it will be helpful to consider briefly such ideas as knowing and helping the learner, the nature of learning, and the cooperative tasks of the leader and the group members.

KNOWING AND HELPING THE LEARNER

The *image* that a young person or adult has of himself is that he is a mature and responsible person. Whether this self-image is accurate or not, he desires to be considered an adult and wants to be treated like one. He is able to and wants to make his own decisions, and must do so. He does not want to be treated as a child, a person still in the dependent stage. The leader, therefore, will want to teach in such a manner that the learner is given opportunity to make his own decisions, recognizing that to learn effectively a person must take responsibilities and be actively involved in the teaching-learning process.

The young person or adult has had *many varied experiences* which have strongly influenced his life. These experiences have made deep impressions upon his personal makeup and have shaped his ways of thinking. He therefore reacts to situations, new ideas, and new meanings in the light of these experiences. The leader will want to consider these as having worth to the individual, allow him to share them without feeling threatened by ridicule or mass group opinion, and make them meaningful to him in new situations. In this way the experiences become an avenue for opening new areas of understanding.

The *atmosphere* of the teaching-learning situation will affect the teaching-learning process. It is important to accept each individual as a person of worth even when one does not agree with his ideas. A concern for his welfare will more easily enable him to evaluate facts and to accept change instead of putting up defenses when new ideas are presented.

Persons are more important than the information to be learned or the way of teaching that is used. Any factual information is useless unless it is of value to the individual and makes a difference in his life. Information should be used to assist the individual to become more mature, not to enslave him with an accumulation of many unrelated, unmeaningful facts. What happens to the individual learner is the important thing.

An atmosphere of trust, security, and mutual confidence must exist so that the learner will feel free to express his ideas honestly. By accepting each learner as a person of worth, the leader will first give support to him and then assist him progressively to accept himself and to understand why he behaves as he does; then, if necessary, the leader will move to a direct challenge of the learner's beliefs. An abrupt challenge to an insecure individual may retard learning or spoil opportunities for learning to take place.

THE NATURE OF LEARNING

Learning involves change. The changes that take place when learning occurs have a directional aspect. Sometimes they involve a change in the direction of life's goals, and sometimes they reinforce the direction in which the learner is going.

When the change involves a complete about-face in our way of thinking, this involves a change in the goal and the direction of our lives. What we did before, we no longer do.

When learning experiences continue to lead us in the same

direction in which we have been going, they give us new insights into and help us to see more clearly the way in which we have been going. This process assists us in advancing more quickly and more clearly toward our goal.

When Paul said, "How changed are my ambitions," [1] he spoke of a change of direction in his life's goals. Once his ambitions were changed, there was a constant growth in the direction of Christian maturity. "I do not consider myself to have 'arrived,' spiritually," he stated, "nor do I consider myself already perfect. But I keep going on, grasping ever more firmly that purpose for which Christ Jesus grasped me." [2] Here is an illustration of strengthening one's continued growth in the same direction.

Learning takes place when the following changes occur: (1) addition of information, (2) increase in understandings, (3) acceptance of new attitudes, (4) acquisition of new appreciations, and (5) doing something with what has been learned.[3] These five kinds of changes fall into three categories: *knowing, feeling,* and *doing.* These involve: (1) what I add to what I already know, (2) how I feel about what I hear and read, and (3) what I do with what I hear and read.

1. What I add to what I already know may have the least impact upon me as an individual. It may have a very comfortable effect as I gloat over and bask in the increase of information. However, while the multiplication of information is important, satisfying, and sometimes even exhilarating, it is only the beginning of the learning process. When additional information has been secured, I need to ask myself the following questions:

(a) What has happened to me because I have this new information?

(b) How does this information assist me to help myself and others?

(c) What kind of person am I because I have this added information?

---

[1] J. B. Phillips, *The New Testament in Modern English* (New York: The Macmillan Company, 1958), Philippians 3:10. Copyright J. B. Phillips 1958. Used by permission of The Macmillan Company and Geoffrey Bles Ltd.

[2] *Ibid.,* Philippians 3:12.

[3] Points adapted from Malcolm S. Knowles, *Informal Adult Education* (New York: Association Press, 1950), pp. 30-31.

(d) Am I in the process of becoming a more effective Christian because of these new insights?

(e) How is the Holy Spirit working in my life so that this information is making me more adequate for the tasks of today in this fast-changing world?

2. *How I feel about what I hear and read* is more important than the mere gaining of information. Our emotional reactions to facts, information, and ideas are important for learning. How we feel about new information or new ideas will determine whether or not we will learn. When we hear new ideas and are unwilling to consider them in the light of valid evidence, it would be well to ask ourselves the following questions:

(a) Why do I keep my mind closed to new information? Is it because I am afraid of myself and new situations? Is it because I do not feel confident enough as a person to be able to meet new situations? Is it because I feel insignificant so that I close my mind when new situations confront me?

(b) Am I reacting to a person or to preconceived prejudices rather than to the new idea or new information? Would the same information given by someone else or said in a different way make a difference in whether I accept it?

(c) Am I allowing the Holy Spirit to work in me to help me in my attitudes toward others so that I may love more, be more patient, be more understanding, and therefore be more open to new insights into God's Word and his ways in my life?

3. *What I do with what I hear and read* is the most important aspect of learning. My exposure to and subsequent acceptance of new ideas should result in overt action. I must become a different person by assimilating what I have heard and expressing it in action. This is the final result of the kind of learning which affects conduct.

For example, I may hear about giving to missions and I may think and even say that this is good; however, I have not really learned to give until I actually share my own possessions. Or I may hear about loving others and give verbal assent to the idea, but the final and necessary step is to show love.

Jesus demanded action of his followers when he said, "Not every one who says to me, 'Lord, Lord,' shall enter the kingdom of heaven, but he who does the will of my Father who is in heaven." [4] After telling the parable of the good Samaritan, he turned to the lawyer and commanded, "Go and do." [5] Moreover, Jesus demonstrated with his life what he taught with words. To be Christian means to live what we hear and believe.

Allowing the Holy Spirit to work in our lives enables us to respond to new insights into God's ways. When the Spirit works he "produces in human life fruits such as these: love, joy, peace, patience, kindness, generosity, fidelity, tolerance and self-control." [6] Learning takes place when the fruits of the Spirit are in evidence.

THE COOPERATIVE TASK

The teaching-learning process is a cooperative effort in which not only the leader but also the group members must be involved as active participants if learning is to take place. Both the leader and the group members are learners, but the leader, with additional knowledge and experience, plays a different role as a learner.

The leader of a group cannot expect response from the members unless he fulfills certain conditions and assists the learners at certain points, while the group member has certain rightful expectations of his leader and also must know the responsibility that he himself must personally assume if genuine learning is to take place. The leader is as responsible to teach group members *how* to learn as he is to teach them *what* to learn. Unless the learner knows what is expected of him he cannot be expected to assume his responsibility as a learner.

For every activity in which the leader participates there is a corresponding activity towards which the group member must consciously strive. Without this two-way effort, significant learning cannot take place.

Some of the important interactions between the leader and group member are these:

THE LEADER is a teacher and a ◄──► THE GROUP MEMBER is a learner learner. and a teacher.

---

[4] Matthew 7:21.
[5] Luke 10:25-37.
[6] Phillips, *op. cit.*, Galatians 5:22-23.

THE LEADER is honest with himself ◄► THE GROUP MEMBER is honest and others. with himself and others.

THE LEADER realizes that how he ◄► THE GROUP MEMBER is sensitive says something is just as impor- to the inflections of the voice and tant as what he says. manners of the leader, and responds appropriately.

THE LEADER knows the group ◄► THE GROUP MEMBER shares with member with whom he is working. the leader as much information as he is ready to share.

THE LEADER is sensitive to the ◄► THE GROUP MEMBER assists the group member's felt and real needs. leader in making his needs known.

THE LEADER remembers that learn- ◄► THE GROUP MEMBER understands ing is a personal matter, and that how significant learning takes the group member learns only place, knows his part in this pro- what he wants to learn. He assists cess, and assumes his responsibility in motivating the learner to see in the teaching-learning process. his potentials and how to achieve them.

THE LEADER never does something ◄► THE GROUP MEMBER never relies for a group member that that per- on the leader to do anything for son can do for himself. him that he himself can do.

THE LEADER is a guide to the ◄► THE GROUP MEMBER accepts the group member and gives direc- leader as a guide who is assisting tion only when needed. him in becoming a more mature person.

THE LEADER assists the group ◄► THE GROUP MEMBER assumes the member in making his own de- responsibility of making his own cisions. decisions and does not leave it to another person to make them for him.

THE LEADER does not expect any- ◄► THE GROUP MEMBER does not al- one to do something which he low the leader to "use" him for himself is not willing to do. his own means.

THE LEADER develops good *rap- ◄► THE GROUP MEMBER accepts the port* with the group member. leader as a person with feelings.

20

THE LEADER is a good listener.	THE GROUP MEMBER is an active listener and participant.
THE LEADER interacts with the group member.	THE GROUP MEMBER interacts with the leader.
THE LEADER has empathy toward the group member.	THE GROUP MEMBER has empathy toward the leader.
THE LEADER is patient when progress is slow, recognizing that progress takes place when group members are ready to progress and not before.	THE GROUP MEMBER consciously tries to understand what is being taught and to progress as rapidly as he can to achieve his goal. He assumes the responsibility for learning.
THE LEADER helps the group member to express himself and is sensitive to the right time to assist him.	THE GROUP MEMBER learns to accept the leader's assistance in developing self-confidence and self-expression.
THE LEADER helps the group member to mature, realizing that he must begin where the group member is and assist him in taking progressive steps toward maturity.	THE GROUP MEMBER knows that learning produces progress toward maturity. He accepts the leader as a person who is assisting him to mature.
THE LEADER never puts the group member on the defensive.	THE GROUP MEMBER learns to recognize when he is defensive.
THE LEADER never reacts defensively to anything that the group member says.	THE GROUP MEMBER never puts the leader on the defensive.
THE LEADER is flexible when the occasion demands.	THE GROUP MEMBER learns to recognize when the leader is assisting him.
THE LEADER challenges the group member when the group member is secure enough to be exposed to new ideas.	THE GROUP MEMBER accepts the challenge, looks at all alternatives, discovers and explores ideas in new relationships, makes his own decisions and is able to defend them.

THE LEADER gives the group member an opportunity to participate in developing the goals of the teaching-learning situation. ◄─► THE GROUP MEMBER assumes his responsibility in determining goals.

THE LEADER helps the group member to strive for goals of *feeling* and *doing* as soon as possible. ◄─► THE GROUP MEMBER involves himself in goals of *knowing, feeling,* and *doing,* and moves to the *feeling* and *doing* goals as soon as possible.

THE LEADER exposes the group member to significant facts and resources that are relevant to achieving the goals set. ◄─► THE GROUP MEMBER reacts to what the leader says or to the resources the leader uses in relation to the group member's own past knowledge, and tries to relate it to his experiences in such a way that it has meaning.

THE LEADER selects and provides proper resources and ways to attain the goals set. ◄─► THE GROUP MEMBER learns to select resources and ways that will assist him in achieving the goals which he has helped to set.

THE LEADER gives the group member opportunities to assume responsibilities for the teaching-learning situation. He is sensitive to the times when the group member is ready and needs a little encouragement. ◄─► THE GROUP MEMBER accepts responsibilities for the teaching-learning situation according to his readiness.

THE LEADER constantly evaluates himself. ◄─► THE GROUP MEMBER constantly evaluates himself.

THE LEADER evaluates the group member's performance at frequent intervals so that the group member will know his progress. ◄─► THE GROUP MEMBER applies himself to new learnings and assimilates them into his thinking so that he can communicate them to others.

THE LEADER evaluates the atmosphere of the teaching-learning situation. ◄─► THE GROUP MEMBER realizes his responsibility in establishing a positive atmosphere for learning to take place.'

THE LEADER requests at appropri- ⟷ THE GROUP MEMBER is honest
ate intervals, evaluations from the in his evaluations of the teaching-
group members concerning the learning situation, reporting exact-
strengths and weaknesses of the ly how he reacts to what is going
teaching-learning situation. on, giving praise where it is valid
and constructive criticism where it
is warranted.

THE LEADER is willing to adjust ⟷ THE GROUP MEMBER is co-
the teaching-learning process in operative in making adjustments in
accordance with the evaluative the teaching-learning situation.
comments of the group member.

In a group learning situation, the interrelationships that must
exist between the leader and the group member are the same
relationships that the learners or group members must assume
between themselves and other learners.

2.
which way is best for me?

WHICH OF THE FORTY WAYS to teach is the most appropriate for a specific situation? The answer depends upon many factors, ten of which are considered in this chapter. Some of them may at first seem to restrict greatly the choice of teaching methods, but on closer examination the restrictions will appear to be minimal.

THE GOALS TO BE ACHIEVED

A specific way of teaching has no value in and of itself. It is useful only insofar as it helps to achieve a specific, worthy purpose.

1. Who determines the goals? Whenever possible, the goals should be determined cooperatively by the leader and the group members. The possibility of achieving the goals is directly proportionate to the extent to which they are determined by the group members.

2. How are the goals to be stated? Goals should be listed in terms of the desired changes to be sought and achieved. We have already considered three kinds of changes that are desirable: changes in knowing, feeling, and doing. It is important to know the kinds of changes that are desired and to provide a proper balance among them.

Changes in knowing. If the desired changes are to be in the form of additional information or increased understandings, we are dealing with the category of "knowing'" behavior. For instance, if a group of persons is preparing an educational experience under the topic "How Do Persons Behave in Groups?" an example of a "knowledge" goal would be "to acquire information about the various kinds of behavior that persons display in a group."

Changes in feeling. If the desired changes are to be in the form of the acceptance of new attitudes or the acquisition of new appreciations, we are dealing with the category of "feelings." Using the same topic as above, an example of a goal involving feelings would be "to develop an attitude of concern for other people in a group."

Changes in doing. If the desired changes are to be in the form of putting into action what one has learned, we are dealing with the category of "doing" or "overt action." Again using the same topic as listed above, an example of a goal involving overt action would be "to assist others with their problems of communicating."

In all three kinds of changes listed above, the infinitive form of the verb is crucial. In the illustrations given, the desired "knowing" action is "to acquire information"; the desired "feeling" action is "to develop an attitude"; and the desired "doing" action is "to assist."

Since changes in the learner take place when learning occurs, the above goals have been stated in terms of the kinds of changes that are desired *by the learner.* Too often leaders develop goals that are listed in terms of what the teacher is to do. For example, when a goal is listed as being "*to assist the student* in acquiring information about the various kinds of behavior persons display in a group," it is stated in terms of the activity desired by the teacher. Although it is important for the teacher to have goals, we are here interested in what is to happen to students and how they can become involved. Therefore, we state the goal in terms of the learner: "*to acquire* information about the various kinds of behavior people display in groups." When the goal is thus stated in terms of the learners, and they have assisted in determining the goal, there is more possibility that it will be reached.

3. *Which way(s) to select?* It is not easy to determine which way(s) would be best to achieve a particular goal. This kind of wisdom comes with experience and discernment. In any case, a leader or group must learn to use their best judgment.

Many of the ways would assist in achieving all three kinds of changes; some would assist in achieving only two kinds of changes; and a few would achieve only one kind of change. Most of the ways, however, would point toward a predominant emphasis on one kind. The following list suggests ways that would most likely bring about predominant changes in each.

KNOWING	FEELING	DOING
Book Report	Brainstorming	Demonstration-Work
Lecture	Buzz Groups	Group
Panel	Case Study	Field Trip
Questions and Answers	Chain-Reaction Forum	Work Groups
Research and Report	Circle Response	Workshop
Screened Speech	Colloquy	
Symposium	Couple Buzzers	
Symposium Dialogue	Debate Forum	
	Depth Bible	
	Encounter	
	Expanding Panel	
	Film Talk-Back	
	Gallery Conversations	
	Group Discussion	
	Group Drawing	
	Group Response	
	Team	
	Group Writing	
	Inductive Bible Study	
	Interview Forum	
	Lecture Forum	
	Listening Teams	
	Music Forum	
	Panel Forum	
	Play-Reading	
	Talk-Back	
	Reaction Panel	
	Role-Playing	
	Seminar	
	Sermon Forum	
	Symposium Forum	

Remember that changes which produce action in living are our chief purpose for learning. The ways that emphasize feelings would be more likely to produce changes in overt action than the ways that emphasize only the accumulation of knowledge.

THE SIZE OF THE GROUP

1. The small group (fifteen persons or less). Changes in persons are more likely to take place in an atmosphere of interaction between the teacher and the pupils where there is opportunity for give-and-take in the clarification and expansion of ideas.

When we consider the number of relationships which take place among persons in various-sized groups, some conclusions can be drawn. Note the following diagram.

As the diagram shows, when three people are involved in conversation, there is a pattern of six interpersonal relationships. When four persons are communicating, the number of interpersonal relationships increases to twelve. As the number of people in a group increases, the number of interpersonal relationships increases geometrically to form the following equation: the number of relationships *(r)* equals the number of persons in the group *(n)* multiplied by one less than the number of persons in the group *(n-1)*. This formula may be expressed in the equation $r = n(n-1)$. Try this on the diagram above.

Thus it is evident that the larger the group the less possibility there is of interpersonal relationships among the participants. When a group exceeds fifteen persons, the number of members who are able to participate meaningfully would be limited. A very few aggressive members would tend to dominate the discussion in a larger group. Because of this, many churches have disbanded their large organized classes in favor of smaller interest groups.

The ways that are especially adapted for the smaller groups are:

Case Study	Field Trip	Music Forum
Circle Response	Group Discussion	Seminar
Expanding Panel	Inductive Bible Study	

2. *The large group* (over fifteen persons). It is obvious that the ways most appropriate for larger groups would be those where only one-way communication takes place, or where the audience is divided into smaller groups before or after some means of general presentation of information. These would include:

Chain-Reaction Forum	Group Response Team	Sermon Forum Workshop
Colloquy	Reaction Panel	

3. *Any sized group.* Some ways can be used in either the large or small groups. These are as follows:

Book Report	Gallery Conversations	Play-Reading
Brainstorming	Group Drawing	Talk-Back
Buzz Groups	Group Writing	Questions and Answers
Couple Buzzers	Interview Forum	Research and Report
Debate Forum	Lecture	Role-Playing
Demonstration-Work Group	Lecture Forum	Screened Speech
Depth Bible Encounter	Listening Teams	Symposium
	Panel	Symposium Dialogue
Film Talk-Back	Panel Forum	Symposium Forum
		Work Groups

THE SIZE OF THE ROOM

C. Harry Atkinson recommends a minimum of eight square feet of floor space to be allotted for every adult in a learning group.[1] He recommends from eight to ten square feet per person for more formal types of learning experiences, and from ten to twelve square feet per person for the activity types of teaching. This also would be a minimum for young people.

The approximate amount of room space to be allotted for the various ways of teaching and learning are arranged below for convenient use. When more than one way is used in one session, it is important to provide room for the one which demands the

[1] Harry C. Atkinson, *Building and Equipping for Christian Education.* (New York: National Council of the Churches of Christ in the U.S.A., Revised Edition 1963), p. 51.

largest floor space. For example, if plans for a session include both lecture forum (8-9 square feet) and work groups (10-12 square feet), it is the latter amount of space that should be provided for the entire session.

From 8 to 9 square feet per person	*From 9 to 10 square feet per person*	*From 10 to 12 square feet per person*
Book Report	Buzz Groups	Chain-Reaction
Brainstorming	Case Study	Forum
Couple Buzzers	Circle Response	Colloquy
Field Trip: Steps 1, 3	Debate Forum	Expanding Panel
Interview Forum	Demonstration-Work	Film Talk-Back
Lecture	Group	Group Drawing
Lecture Forum	Depth Bible	Group Writing
Listening Teams	Encounter	Play-Reading
Questions and Answers	Gallery Conversations	Talk-Back
Research and Report	Group Discussion	Role-Playing
	Group Response	Work Groups
	Team	Workshop
	Inductive Bible Study	
	Music Forum	
	Panel	
	Panel Forum	
	Reaction Panel	
	Screened Speech	
	Seminar	
	Sermon Forum	
	Symposium	
	Symposium Dialogue	
	Symposium Forum	

THE TIME AVAILABLE

Some of the ways of teaching developed here call for rather large blocks of time, while others are effective when carried on for only brief periods. Generally speaking, more time is required when the group members are involved in two-way communication than when the leader is predominant. The approximate amount of time needed to carry out each activity is as follows:

10-30 minutes needed

Book Report	Couple Buzzers	Lecture
Brainstorming	Demonstration-Work	Listening Teams
Buzz Groups	Group	Questions and Answers
Circle Response	Interview Forum	Role-Playing

60-75 minutes needed

Case Study
Colloquy [2]
Debate Forum [2]
Depth Bible
Encounter [2]
Expanding Panel
Film Talk-Back [2]
Gallery Conversations
Group Discussion [2]

Group Drawing [2]
Group Response
Team
Group Writing [2]
Inductive Bible
Study [2]
Lecture Forum
Music Forum
Panel
Panel Forum [2]

Play-Reading
Talk-Back [2]
Reaction Panel
Research and Report
Screened Speech
Symposium
Symposium Dialogue [2]
Symposium Forum [2]
Work Groups [2]

60-90 minutes needed

Chain-Reaction Forum
Seminar

1½ to 2 hours needed

Sermon Forum

An extended period of time needed

Field Trip
Workshop

THE FACILITIES AVAILABLE

Never limit your teaching to the lecture method because you teach in a room with immovable chairs or in the church sanctuary with pews. Thirty of the forty ways of teaching described here can be used under such conditions.

Eight of these thirty ways are more suitable in a room with movable chairs but can be adapted to permanent seating. For example, when buzz groups are desirable to secure small-group response, it is advisable to rearrange chairs so that each group is seated in a circle. However, where learners are seated in pews, the pews can be numbered. Those persons sitting in the odd-numbered pews can be requested to turn around and speak to those sitting directly behind them in the even-numbered pews. In this situation, it is advisable to have only four persons in each buzz group, and to keep the time of the buzz session at a minimum.

The following lists suggest which ways are usable under certain circumstances. It should always be remembered, however, that the best atmosphere for teaching comes from informal rooms and adaptable equipment.

[2] In some situations a longer period of time may be needed.

In a room with immovable chairs or pews [3]

Book Report
Brainstorming
Buzz Groups [4]
Case Study
  (individual or entire
  group)
Colloquy
Couple Buzzers
Debate Forum
Demonstration-Work
  Group (Step 1)
Depth Bible
  Encounter [4]

Field Trip
  (Steps 1, 3)
Film Talk-Back [4]
Group Response
  Team
Interview Forum
Lecture
Lecture Forum
Listening Teams [4]
Music Forum [4]
Panel
Panel Forum
Play-Reading
  Talk-Back [4]

Questions and Answers
Reaction Panel
Research and Report
  (Individual)
Role-Playing [4]
Screened Speech [4]
Sermon Forum
  (Steps 1, 3)
Symposium
Symposium Dialogue
Symposium Forum
Workshop (Step 1)

One table needed for entire group

Group Discussion
Seminar

Numerous tables needed for small-group work

Case Study
  (work groups)
Chain-Reaction
  Forum
Demonstration-Work
  Group (Step 2)

Group Drawing
Group Writing
Inductive Bible
  Study

Research and Report
  (group work)
Work Groups
Workshop (Step 2)

Table needed for panel and movable chairs for all participants

Expanding Panel

Flexible chair arrangement desirable with no tables needed

Circle Response   Gallery Conversations   Sermon Forum (Step 2)

In all teaching situations, a chalkboard or newsprint pad should be available for ready use.

THE RESOURCES AVAILABLE

Some communities have more resources available than others, but few teachers use all those which are at their disposal.

[3] Tables or a podium will be needed for speaker, panel, etc.
[4] More desirable when used in a room where chairs are movable.

In fact, some teachers have not explored, and are not aware of, available resources near at hand.

Resources may include educational aids such as audio-visual materials, a large variety of printed materials, and various resource persons. Be sure that you fully explore the resources of the people within your own group. Whenever possible, use the group members as resource persons.

No matter what kinds of resources are used, it is necessary to plan well in advance for their use. Thus it takes time to provide for special resources, but the time put into this preparation usually brings worthwhile results.

The following lists suggest the kinds of resources needed for some of the ways to teach that are developed in this book.

Resources needed	*Ways to teach*
Film and projectionist	Film Talk-Back
Information briefs	Case Study Questions and Answers (when a list is prepared by the leader)
Pictures or sculpture	Gallery Conversations
Play and readers	Play-Reading Talk-Back
Recordings	Music Forum
Resource books	Depth Bible Encounter Inductive Bible Study Research and Report Seminar
Special equipment which varies according to needs	Demonstration-Work Group Group Drawing Group Writing Work Groups Workshop

Resource persons
    (Experts who respond to
    needs of group without
    a prepared speech)
	Chain-Reaction Forum
	Colloquy
	Expanding Panel
	Field Trip
	Interview Forum
	Panel

Resources needed	*Ways to teach*
	Panel Forum
Resource persons	Reaction Panel (Step 2)
(continued)	Screened Speech
	Symposium Dialogue (Step 2)
	Workshop
Speaker(s) with prepared	Debate Forum
speech(es)	Group Response Team (Step 1)
	Lecture
	Lecture Forum
	Reaction Panel (Step 1)
	Sermon Forum (Step 1)
	Symposium
	Symposium Dialogue (Step 1)
	Symposium Forum

THE PROXIMITY OF OTHER GROUPS

Some study groups meet in locations which are not conducive to the best educational results, but until improvements are possible, teachers must make the best of the situation. In churches where several groups meet simultaneously in a church sanctuary, or only have a light curtain or divider to separate them from their neighbors, limitations in using some of the ways to teach do exist, but these are less rigid than most people realize.

The ways which no doubt *could not* be used when noise is a factor are the Chain-Reaction Forum, Film Talk-Back, Music Forum, Sermon Forum, and Workshop. Rather than deciding that these ways of teaching cannot be used, however, explore the possibility of an additional time of meeting that would allow for their use.

THE AGE OF GROUP MEMBERS

As age increases, the rate of mobility declines. As the bodily functions slow down, it takes longer to perform tasks. This limitation does not affect the kinds of activities possible for older adults as much as it affects the rate of speed at which such activities can be performed.

Many older adults prefer to continue familiar ways of doing things, but some will surprise you by their positive reaction to new ways of teaching. The important thing is that there should be a feeling of accomplishment and achievement at the end of the learning experience.

THE CLIMATE OF THE GROUP

The cultural, ethnic, educational, psychological, sociological, and spiritual climate of the group will partly determine the ways to be used in teaching. It is therefore important for the teacher to know the students. He should know them well, and know what their expectations are. When he knows their expectations he can begin where the students are, and after he has developed their confidence and trust the group will accept some of the newer ways.

Remember, however, that some groups will be immediately ready for new ways, for they are tired of being "talked at" and "talked to."

THE TEACHER

Are you the kind of a teacher who is afraid to try something new? Do you feel safer and more secure when you follow the way that you have always followed? If you give in to this feeling you may think that you are helping yourself, but instead you are harming the group. Actually you are not even helping yourself; you are stunting your own growth.

It is true that every time you try a new way you are taking a kind of risk. It is a risk worth taking, however. If a new way of teaching is well planned and well executed, its use will be rewarding to you and to the members of the group. And if it doesn't succeed the first time — try again! If the group is planning and working with you, and you are letting them assume their share of responsibility, they will be able to help you decide how to do better next time.

Don't let yourself be a hindrance to another person's learning!

CHOOSING WHICH WAYS TO USE

After determining what factors may assist or limit your use of certain ways of teaching, you will be ready to plan specifically for your teaching session. The following six-step procedure for planning suggested by John McKinley and Robert Smith[5] is

[5] John McKinley and Robert M. Smith, *Guide to Program Planning: A Handbook* (New York: The Seabury Press, 1965).

worthy of consideration and use. The order of the six steps is very important.

1. Find an interest or need.
2. Determine a topic or topics related to the interest or need.
3. Set goals that you wish to accomplish.
4. Survey the available resources.
5. Select the appropriate way(s) to achieve the goals.
6. Outline the session and assign responsibilities.

Note that the ways to use in teaching should not be selected until the needs, topics, goals, and resources are determined. The way chosen has validity only as a means to achieve the desired goal with the aid of available resources at one's disposal.

In advance of any meeting, certain responsibilities must be cared for by the leader or by other persons whom he designates. Such preparations include proper lighting, adequate ventilation, a room arrangement which is appropriate to the way to be used, and provision for the comfort of the group members.

3.

the forty ways to teach

IN THE FOLLOWING PAGES, forty separate ways to teach have been outlined. It is important, however, to realize that in many sessions it is suitable, and often advisable, to combine as many as three or four ways in various orderings. The teacher who uses his imagination creatively and does not fear to experiment will find interesting combinations of ways to assist students in becoming involved in the teaching-learning process through a variety of group relationships.

More than one hundred different combinations are possible, so there is a challenge for you to help members of your group to learn in an exciting atmosphere of acceptance, openness, and exploration of new insights.

WHAT DO THE DIAGRAMS SAY?

Each description of a way to teach is accompanied by a diagram. Study these carefully. In every teaching-learning situation there are certain forces at work involving interaction between people. In some groups only the teacher or leader speaks, and the individuals in the class do not have any opportunity to respond by asking questions or giving opinions. In a situation such as this we can say that there is no overt interaction between the leader and the group members; there is only *one-way* communication. This kind of teaching-learning situation is diagrammed as shown on the next page.

In another situation where the learner or group member is encouraged to ask questions or to contribute ideas, the direction of communication is *two-way*. Persons are allowed and encouraged to react verbally to what is said. This pattern of communication is diagrammed as follows:

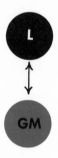

When members of the group are free to address questions or comments to other members as well as to the leader, arrows link the group members to each other as well as to the leader.

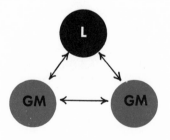

The arrows in each diagram show the direction of communication. The letters inside the circles indicate the following:

L = leader
GM = group member
GR = group representative
RP = resource person
PM = panel member
S = speaker
R = reader
P = pastor

EVALUATION IS IMPORTANT

After each description of a way of teaching, the suggestions end with evaluation of the learning experience. This is included to help you keep in mind the importance of such evaluation. You will find helpful answers to some questions about evaluation beginning on page 117. Be sure you do not let this part of the session become stereotyped. Plan for varying the ways to be used for individual and group evaluation, depending upon the needs and possibilities of each session.

1. BOOK REPORT

One person summarizes and interprets the thoughts of an author.

The Goal: To gain information.

The Leader

1. Reads the book.
2. Asks questions about what the author is saying.
3. Outlines significant points of interest.
4. Determines how the information can best be conveyed to the listeners.

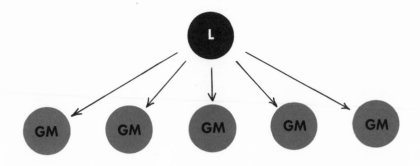

5. Presents key ideas conversationally to the group.

The Group Members

1. Listen actively.
2. Associate the meaning with previous experiences.
3. Identify new ideas and integrate these into their thinking.
Note: Some books lend themselves to the reporter's presenting the contents in the first person. This is especially true for a historical or autobiographical book. In some cases appropriate dress will add color to the presentation.

2. BRAINSTORMING

The leader presents a problem to members of the group, who in reply suggest solutions to the problem. The suggestions are recorded on a chalkboard or newsprint as the group members offer them in rapid succession, allowing no comments or criticisms. After the list is completed, the suggested solutions are evaluated by the group or a committee.

The Goal: To secure many possible solutions to a problem.

The Leader

1. Introduces the problem or issue facing the group.
2. Appoints a secretary to record the suggestions offered by members of the group.
3. Presents the following ground rules for the group members:
   a. Give suggested solutions in rapid succession.
   b. Give any ideas that come to your mind.
   c. Avoid evaluating individual comments.
4. Designates the length of time the brainstorming is to continue.
5. Requests suggestions for solutions.
6. Appoints a committee to evaluate suggestions and determine how these suggestions can be put into effect, or leads the group in such evaluation.

The Group Members

1. Think intently.
2. Present *any* ideas that come to their minds regardless of how ridiculous these may seem.
3. Refrain from commenting, positively or negatively, on any suggestions made by other group members.
4. Assist in evaluating suggestions when the brainstorming session is over.
5. Determine how this information is to be used and put into action.
6. Assist in evaluating the group's learning experience.

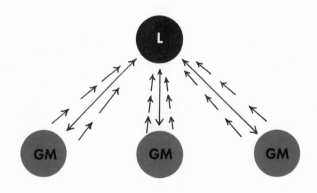

Resources

Bergevin and others, *Adult Education Procedures*, pp. 195-196.
Clark, *Brainstorming*, entire book.
Ford, *A Primer for Teachers and Leaders*, pp. 78-79.

3. BUZZ GROUPS

A group is divided into subgroups of from three to six persons each for a brief period of time, to discuss an assigned topic or to solve a problem. A representative is sometimes selected from each subgroup to report its findings to the entire group.

The Goal: To gain information; to solve a problem or discuss an issue.

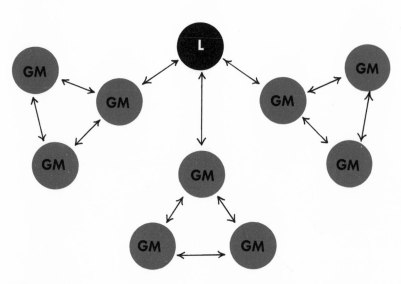

The Leader

1. Assists in determinining the issue or problem.
2. Depending upon the size of the group and the space available, divides the group into subgroups of from three to six persons.
3. Gives instructions to the subgroups:
   a. Defines the task clearly.
   b. Informs the group members of the time limit (from five to fifteen minutes) to accomplish the task.
   c. Suggests that each subgroup select its own leader and recorder.
4. Requests suggestions for solving the problem, clarifying the issue, or answering the question.
5. Floats from one group to another to determine whether any group needs assistance in performing its task.
6. Gives a two-minute warning signal for subgroups to terminate their task.
7. Calls time for the subgroups to reassemble.
8. Requests a report from each subgroup, to be given by its recorder.
9. Requests any additional comments from any member of the group.
10. Summarizes the findings of the group, or suggests that someone else do it.
11. Proposes additional study or action.
12. Evaluates the strengths and weaknesses of the learning situation.

The Group Members

1. Assist in determining the issue or problem facing them.
2. Help select a leader and recorder in each subgroup.
3. Restate and define the issue or problem.
4. Give suggestions for discussing the issue or solving the problem.
5. Listen intently and appreciatively to the other group members' contributions.
6. Build upon the contributions of other persons.
7. Determine how this information is to be used and put into action.

8. Assist in evaluating the effectiveness of the learning experience.

The Recorders

1. Record all contributions in their subgroup.
2. Summarize the contributions of the subgroup.
3. Report the findings of the subgroup.

Alternate Suggestions

1. In a large group not all subgroups need to report.
2. It may not be necessary for any reports of subgroups to be given. The discussion in the subgroups may be adequate.

Resources

Bergevin and others, *Adult Education Procedures*, pp. 191-196.
Caldwell, *Adults Learn and Like It*, pp. 60-62.
Thelen, *Dynamics of Groups at Work*, pp. 201-210.

4. CASE STUDY

Information regarding a real life situation is presented to the group members, who analyze all the aspects of the problem and offer a solution.

The Goal: To analyze and solve a problem.

The Leader

1. Prepares the case study, recording information factually, accurately, and objectively, considering the following relevant facts:
   a. The people involved.
   b. The historical background of the situation.
   c. The relationships among persons or groups involved.
   d. The religious background and perspective of the situation.

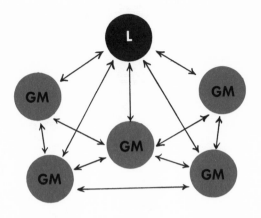

e. The sociological factors involved.
f. The economic factors involved.
g. The educational backgrounds of persons involved.
h. The ethnic origins of the persons involved.
i. The tensions causing the problem.
2. Assists group members in analyzing and solving the problem.
3. Summarizes the findings of the group, or requests someone else to do it.
4. Suggests a course of action or a way of using the information.
5. Evaluates the group's learning experience.

The Group Members

1. Assist in preparing the case study, if requested.
2. Read or listen to the case study carefully and analytically.
3. Determine what the real issues are.
4. Determine how each person contributes to the problem.
5. Determine why the problem exists.
6. Determine what biblical, theological, psychological, sociological, and educational principles might assist in understanding the situation and suggesting a solution.
7. Suggest all possible solutions, analyzing the pros and cons of each suggestion.
8. Suggest what they consider the best solution to the problem, giving adequate reasons for their choice.
9. Assist in evaluating the group's learning experience.

Note: The case study may be analyzed by each individual in the group or may be analyzed by small subgroups.

Resources

Edge, *Teaching for Results*, pp. 136-143.
Fallaw, *The Case Method in Pastoral and Lay Education*, entire book.

5. CHAIN-REACTION FORUM

A group is divided into subgroups which are assigned to different aspects of a major controversial problem to be discussed. Each subgroup appoints a quizzer, a heckler, and a summarizer. Questions formulated by each subgroup are then presented to panel members by the quizzers and hecklers. At the conclusion of the session, the summarizers give a brief summary of the findings of their groups' assigned areas.

The Goal: To consider a systematic presentation of a controversial issue: to seek a solution for the issue.

The Leader

1. Assists in selecting a controversial problem to be discussed by the group.
2. Analyzes the problem to determine from four to six major issues involved.
3. Prepares the room with as many tables as there are issues.
4. Places the appropriate number of chairs around each table.
5. Places on each table a placard which designates one of the issues to be discussed.
6. Contacts in advance two or three panel members knowledgeable about the subject to be discussed; gives each a list of the issues.
7. Introduces the problem to the entire group.

8. Allows each group member to decide which issue of the problem he would like to discuss.
9. Requests each group member to go to the table where the placard indicates the issue he wishes to discuss.
10. Appoints one person at each table to be the quizzer for his group.
11. Defines the time limit for the group's work.

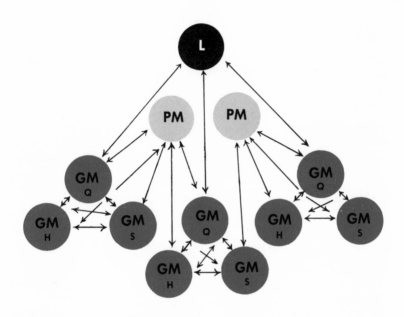

12. Requests each subgroup to select its own heckler and summarizer.
13. Presents to each group a mimeographed sheet explaining the responsibilities of the group and the responsibilities of the quizzer, the heckler, and the summarizer.
14. Floats from group to group to offer help where needed.
15. Gives a two-minute warning signal.
16. Calls time for the groups to complete their tasks and reassemble.

17. Introduces the panel members to the group.
18. Requests the first subgroup to ask the questions prepared by his group and allows each panel member to respond to each question.
19. Acts as moderator of the panel, refraining from giving his own opinions.
20. Requests comments from the heckler of the first subgroup and allows a response from the panel members.
21. Asks each subgroup, in turn, for questions, first from the quizzer and then from the heckler.
22. Requests final comments from each panel member after each subgroup has contributed.
23. Requests a brief statement from each summarizer.
24. Makes a final statement or summary of the session.
25. Suggests further study or course of action.
26. Evaluates the learning experience.

The Group Members

1. Assist in selecting a controversial problem to be discussed.
2. Select the specific issue in which they have most interest.
3. Sit at the table which designates the issue they have chosen.
4. Help select a heckler and summarizer in their subgroup.
5. Contribute questions related to the issue which they have selected.
6. Listen actively to all of the questions that are asked and to the responses of the panel members.
7. Objectively determine the best possible solution to the problem.
8. Determine a course of action or a way of using the information.
9. Assist in evaluating the group's effectiveness.

The Quizzer

1. Acts as the recorder of his subgroup, recording all questions presented by its members.
2. Asks the panel members the questions prepared by his subgroup.

The Heckler

1. Asks additional questions of the panel members, especially

those of a provocative nature; asks for clarification, or makes statements about the topic.

The Summarizer

1. Prepares a fifty- to one-hundred-word summary of the issues involved in his subgroup.
2. Presents this summary to the entire group when requested by the leader.

The Panel Members

1. Meet with the leader prior to the meeting to determine their responsibilities.
2. Consider the listing of problems involved in the issue, as prepared by the leader.
3. Secure relevant facts and interesting information connected with these issues.
4. Answer the questions asked by the quizzers and hecklers.
5. Give a brief summary or additional comments at the end of the panel session.

Resources

Rohrbough and Getsinger, *Adult Leadership,* November, 1957, pp. 131, 140.

6. CIRCLE RESPONSE

The leader proposes a question to members of a group seated in a circle. Each person, in turn, expresses his response. No one is allowed to speak a second time until all have had a turn.

The Goal: To contribute opinions on a problem or issue facing a group; to consider the opinions expressed by others.

The Leader

1. Places the chairs in a circle.
2. Introduces the topic or question to the entire group.

49

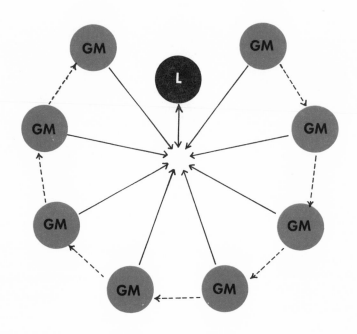

3. Explains that each member will be asked to respond to the question.
4. Requests the person to his left to respond to the question first; then asks each person, in turn, to respond until everyone has had an opportunity to speak.
5. Asks for additional comments from each member or opens the discussion for those who have additional comments to make.
6. Summarizes the group's contributions.
7. Proposes additional study or a course of action.
8. Evaluates the learning experience.

The Group Members

1. Assist in defining the question, being sure that it is understood by all members of the group.
2. Contribute answers to the question asked.
3. Listen intently to the other members' contributions.
4. Identify new ideas and integrate these into their thinking.

5. Determine how the information is to be used.

6. Assist in evaluating the group's effectiveness.

Resources

Little, *Learning Together in the Christian Fellowship,* pp. 49-50.
Planning and Leading Large Meetings, p. 13.

7. COLLOQUY

Three or four persons selected from a group present various aspects of a problem to three or four resource persons who respond to them.

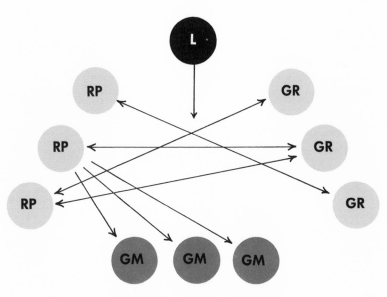

The Goal: To secure information from experts on the problem or issue under consideration, through questioning by representatives of the larger group.

The Leader

1. Places two tables facing one another diagonally in the front of the room, and places the appropriate number of chairs behind each table. Group representatives will sit at one table, and resource persons at the other.
2. Selects resource persons in advance and gives them instructions about their responsibilities.
3. Introduces the problem or issue to the entire group.
4. Requests from the group members suggestions that might solve the problem, clarify the issues, or answer the question.
5. Selects three to four persons from the group to act as group representatives.
6. Acts as moderator of the colloquy as the group representatives ask questions of the resource persons.
7. Requests additional questions from the group as a whole if the time or occasion permits.
8. Summarizes the contributions of the resource persons.
9. Proposes additional study or a course of action.
10. Evaluates the learning experience.

The Leader (Alternate Suggestion)

1. Follows instructions in items one to four above.
2. Divides the group into subgroups of from three to six persons.
3. Requests each subgroup to prepare questions for the resource persons to consider.
4. Follows instructions given in points three to seven in the Buzz Group procedure (see page 42).
5. Selects three to four persons from the group to act as group representatives and gives the questions from the subgroups to them.
6. Follows instructions given in points six to ten above.

The Group Members

1. Restate and define the problem.

2. Help select the leader and the recorder in the subgroups if alternate suggestion is followed.
3. Think intently about the question at hand.
4. Listen actively to the contributions of other group members.
5. Suggest questions to be presented to the resource persons.
6. Associate meanings with previous experiences.
7. Identify new ideas and integrate these into their thinking.
8. Determine a course of action or a way of using the information secured.
9. Assist in evaluating the group's effectiveness.

The Group Representatives

1. Prepare questions to ask the resource persons.
2. If the alternate suggestion is followed, organize the questions prepared by the subgroups, avoiding duplication, and rewording where necessary.

The Resource Persons

1. Meet with the leader prior to the meeting to determine what is expected of them.
2. Clarify the problem or issue to be discussed.
3. Secure relevant facts and interesting information that relate to the problem or issue.
4. Answer the questions asked by the group representatives.
5. Present additional information that is relevant.
6. Briefly summarize their viewpoints as expressed during the colloquy.

Resources

Bergevin, Morris, and Smith, *Adult Education Procedure,* pp. 42-54.
McKinley, *Creative Methods for Adult Classes,* pp. 76-83.

8. COUPLE BUZZERS

A group is divided into couples for a short period of time to discuss an assigned topic or to solve a problem. One member of each couple is chosen to be its spokesman and present the findings to the entire group. When the group is large, only those who desire to report are asked to do so.

The Goal: To discuss a topic or to solve a problem.

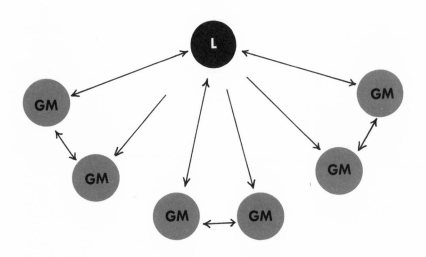

The Leader

1. Assists in determining the problem or issue.
2. Divides the group into subgroups of two persons each.
3. Requests suggestions that might solve the problem, clarify the issue, or answer the question.
4. Defines the time limit for discussion (from five to ten minutes).
5. Gives a one-minute warning signal.
6. Calls time for couples to discontinue discussion.
7. Requests a free discussion of the problem or issue based

upon the small discussion group participation. (When the group is small, the leader requests contributions from each couple.)

8. Summarizes the group's contributions.
9. Proposes areas of additional study or a course of action.
10. Evaluates the learning experience.

The Group Members

1. Assist in determining the problem or issue.
2. Think intently about the question at hand.
3. Associate meanings with previous experiences.
4. Contribute relevant facts and information regarding the problem or issue.
5. Identify new ideas and integrate them into their thinking.
6. Share information with the larger group.
7. Determine a course of action or a way of using the information.
8. Assist in evaluating the group's effectiveness.

9. DEBATE FORUM

Speakers who have opposing views on a controversial subject are given equal time to present the reasons for their beliefs, followed by a free and open discussion of the issue by the entire group.

The Goal: To secure opposing views of a controversial issue; to take part in group reaction to the presentation.

The Leader

1. Places in the front of the room a table with the appropriate number of chairs.
2. Defines the problem to the group members.
3. Acts as moderator for the debating speakers.
4. Opens the topic for free discussion after the debaters have completed their summaries.

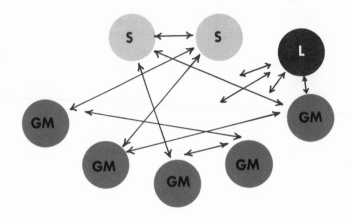

5. Summarizes the contributions which have been made by members of the group.
6. Suggests a course of action or material for additional study.
7. Evaluates the learning experience.

The Group Members

1. Clarify the problem to be discussed.
2. Listen actively to the debating speakers.
3. Participate freely in the discussion after the debate.
4. Evaluate the best course of action.
5. Assist in evaluating the group's effectiveness.

The Debating Speakers

1. Meet with the leader prior to the meeting.
2. Present the issues and propositions.
3. Define terms.
4. Give adequate evidence of their viewpoints.
5. Attack the arguments of their opponents.
6. Defend their own position during the rebuttal.
7. Summarize their position.

Resources

Ford, *A Primer for Teachers and Leaders,* pp. 82-83.
McBurney and Mills, *Argumentation and Debate,* entire book.

10. DEMONSTRATION — WORK GROUP

One or more persons show a group how to carry on certain operations or demonstrate the results of specific procedures or conduct. Opportunity is given to the group members to practice the operations or procedures.

The Goal: To watch or listen to an operation or procedure and to have opportunity to practice it.

The Leader

1. Prepares the room with the proper equipment for the demonstration.
2. Introduces the purpose of the demonstration.
3. Describes the steps of the operation as it is being performed, giving reasons for each step.
4. Defines ways and times for using the procedures.
5. Divides the group into subgroups to carry out the steps which were demonstrated.
6. Summarizes the activities of the session.
7. Proposes action.
8. Evaluates the learning experience.

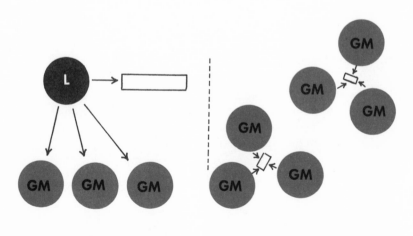

DEMONSTRATION   SUBGROUPS

The Group Members

1. Determine the purpose of the demonstration.
2. Listen actively to the instructions.
3. Think intently about the task at hand.
4. Look carefully at each step of the operation being demonstrated.
5. Ask questions when the information is not clear.
6. Identify new ideas and integrate them into their thinking.
7. Practice the steps of the procedure demonstrated.
8. Determine how they can use this procedure in their own experience.
9. Assist in evaluating the group's effectiveness.

Resources

Bergevin, Morris, and Smith, *Adult Education Procedures,* pp. 63-73.
How to Teach Adults, pp. 37-38.

11. DEPTH BIBLE ENCOUNTER

Each individual writes a Bible verse or passage in his own words, not using any of the words in the Bible text. He shares it with other members of the entire group, or of a subgroup, and they question him about its meaning. Each individual then answers the question, "If I took this passage seriously what would I have to do?" The answers are shared with the other group members.

The Goal: To search one's own life in relation to the teachings of the Bible.

The Leader

1. Assists in selecting a Bible passage to be studied.
2. Requests each person to write out his own paraphrase of the

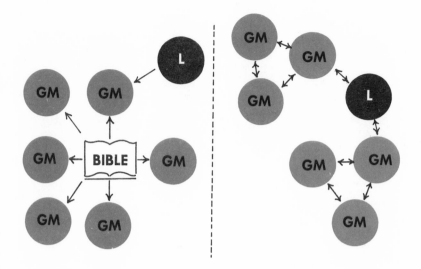

STEP 1   STEP 2

Bible passage, not using any words of the text, and making it approximately the same length as the original passage.
3. Requests each person to answer to himself the question, "What would happen if I took this passage seriously?"
4. Divides the group into subgroups of three to five persons.
5. Presents the following ground rules for the subgroups:
   a. Each person, in turn, shares his paraphrase with the other members of his subgroup, and also shares what he feels would happen if he would take the passage seriously.
   b. Other persons ask questions for clarification to probe into the meaning of the passage.
6. Requests the subgroups to reassemble, and asks one person from each subgroup to share the findings of his group.
7. Summarizes the experiences of the group.
8. Challenges the group to a specific course of action.
9. Evaluates the group's learning experience.

The Group Members

1. Clarify what is expected of them.

2. Think intently about the task at hand.
3. Write out the Bible passage in their own words.
4. Search their own experiences to determine what would happen if they took the passage seriously.
5. Allow the Holy Spirit to guide their thinking.
6. Share their ideas with other members of their subgroup.
7. Revise and clarify their ideas in relation to questions asked by other members of their subgroup.
8. Listen actively when others share their thoughts.
9. Question other persons' ideas when they are not clear.
10. Determine what action to take to carry out what the Holy Spirit is saying to them through the Bible passage.

Resources

Snyder, A. G., *Teaching Adults*, pp. 50-52.
Snyder, R., *Depth and Encounter Study of the Bible.*

12. EXPANDING PANEL

An exploratory discussion of a topic is given by a panel. Then the entire group forms a circle and continues the discussion.

The Goal: To explore an area of interest by gaining the ideas of experts and making these meaningful to one's own experience.

The Leader

1. Places a table in the center of the room, with chairs around the table for the panel members and the leader. Chairs for the group members are placed in a larger circle around the chairs of the panel members.
2. Selects panel members and defines their responsibilities.
3. Defines the problem or issue.
4. Introduces the panel members to the group.
5. Acts as moderator of the panel.

6. Summarizes the contributions of the panel members.
7. Requests the panel members to push their chairs back to join the group members, making one circle.
8. Requests comments or questions from the entire group and encourages free discussion of the topic.
9. Summarizes the expressions of the group.
10. Proposes additional study or a course of action.
11. Evaluates the group's learning experience.

The Group Members

1. Clarify the problem or issue to be discussed.
2. Think intently about the question at hand.
3. Listen actively to the panel members and to the contributions of other group members.
4. Associate meanings with previous experiences.
5. Identify new ideas and integrate these into their thinking.

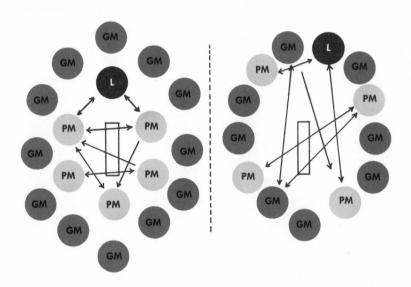

STEP 1   STEP 2

6. Ask questions for clarification.
7. Contribute to the discussion when it is opened to the group members.
8. Determine a course of action or a method of using the additional information.
9. Assist in evaluating the group's learning experiences.

The Panel Members

1. Meet with the leader prior to the meeting to determine their responsibilities.
2. Prepare relevant facts and information regarding the issue to be discussed.
3. Contribute information and opinions on the topic discussed.
4. Build on one another's ideas.
5. Ask for clarification of ideas.
6. Assist in evaluating the learning experience.

Resource

McKinley, *Creative Methods for Adult Classes*, pp. 40-46.

13. FIELD TRIP

The group visits places to observe firsthand sources of information.

The Goal: To gain firsthand experiences with a place of interest or object.

The Leader

STEP 1. PREPARATION FOR THE TRIP
1. Makes all preliminary arrangements with the person(s) in charge of the place to be visited.
2. Describes the purpose of the proposed visit.

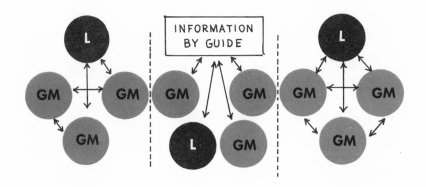

STEP 1	STEP 2	STEP 3

3. Presents relevant data regarding the place to be visited.
4. Presents instructions regarding transportation to the place of interest and decorum to be observed while there.

STEP 2. AT THE PLACE OF INTEREST

5. Introduces the guide to the group members.
6. Is responsible for the group during the tour.

STEP 3. EVALUATION OF THE TRIP

7. Requests the group to report what they saw and heard.
8. Requests the group members to analyze and interpret what they saw and heard.
9. Summarizes the experiences of the group.
10. Suggests a course of action or further study.
11. Evaluates the group's learning experience.

The Group Members

STEP 1

1. Clarify the purpose of the field trip.
2. Listen intently to the instructions given by the leader.
3. Read about the place of interest to be visited.
4. Make preparations for the trip as described by the leader.

STEP 2

5. Keep close to the guide and listen to his explanations.
6. Ask questions of the guide if his explanations are not clear or if additional information is desired.

STEP 3

7. Analyze knowledge gained on the field trip.
8. Interpret knowledge gained on the field trip.
9. Determine a course of action or a way of using the information.
10. Assist in evaluating the learning experience.

Resources

Bergevin, Morris, and Smith, *Adult Education Procedures,* pp. 74-83.
Caldwell, *Adults Learn and Like It,* pp. 85-87.
Clemmons, *Dynamics of Christian Adult Education,* pp. 63-66.

14. FILM TALK-BACK

A film (motion picture or filmstrip) is followed by a time of free, open discussion by the group members.

The Goal: To secure information about a subject of interest to the group; to discuss reactions to the information.

The Leader

1. Arranges the room for good viewing of the screen and provides the proper equipment.
2. Arranges for a projectionist.
3. Introduces the motion picture or filmstrip to the group members.
4. Suggests questions or special items of interest for the group members to consider as they view the film. (Perhaps Listening Teams can be appointed, using the suggestions for these on page 82.)
5. Shows the film to the group members.
6. Leads the group in discussing the questions asked before the

film was shown. (Buzz Groups may be organized before the general discussion, using the suggestions for these on page 42.)

7. Shows the film again if repetition would add to the meaning of its message.
8. Summarizes the contribution of the group members.
9. Suggests further study or a course of action to be taken.
10. Evaluates the group's learning experience.

The Group Members

1. Clarify the purpose of the film to be shown.
2. Clearly understand the questions or items of interest they are asked to consider as they look at the film.
3. Look carefully and listen intently while the film is shown, keeping in mind the questions asked.
4. Analyze what they saw and heard.
5. Share the information they secured from seeing the film.
6. Determine a course of action or a way of using the information gained.
7. Assist in evaluating the group's learning experience.

Resources

Caldwell, *Adults Learn and Like It*, p. 93.
Dialogue with the World, entire book.

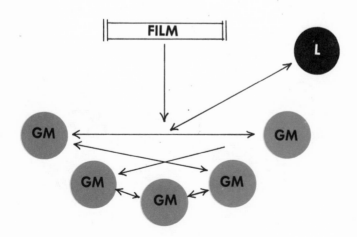

15. GALLERY CONVERSATIONS

An art gallery atmosphere is created by displaying one or more paintings or sculptures about a particular theme, to which a group responds by discussing the meanings which various members find in these.

The Goal: To understand what the artists or sculptors are trying to say through the medium of art.

The Leader

1. Selects a theme for consideration.
2. Selects appropriate pictures or pieces of sculpture, and displays these in appropriate places in the room.
3. Places chairs informally around the display, allowing sufficient space between the chairs and the art selections for the group members to go directly to the art if they desire to view it more closely.
4. Introduces the theme for the display to the group members.
5. Requests the group members to look intently at the display and allows time for them to study it.
6. Asks the question, "What message has this artist (or sculptor) conveyed to you?"
7. Probes more deeply into meanings as the group members give their contributions.

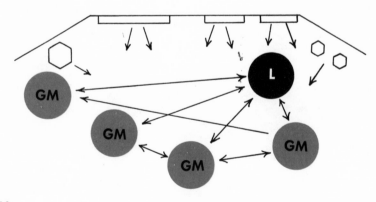

8. Summarizes the contributions of the group members.
9. Suggests a course of action or a way of using the information.
10. Evaluates the group's learning experience.

The Group Members

1. Clarify the theme and purpose of the session.
2. Look intently at the display.
3. Associate meanings with previous experiences.
4. Think intently about the meanings of the art display.
5. Share these meanings with the other group members.
6. Listen to the contributions of the other group members.
7. Build upon one another's contributions.
8. Ask questions to clarify meanings.
9. Consider what difference this experience will make in their lives.
10. Assist in evaluating the group's learning experience.

16. GROUP DISCUSSION

A group of persons meet together with a trained leader to discuss and deliberate cooperatively on a topic of mutual interest.

The Goal: To express opinions and gain information on a topic of interest; to learn from other group members.

The Leader

1. Assists in determining a topic of interest.
2. Encourages group members to do independent research prior to the meeting.
3. Prepares the physical setting, with chairs placed around a table so that all group members face one another.
4. Prepares questions prior to the meeting to open the discussion.
5. Introduces the problem or issue to be discussed.

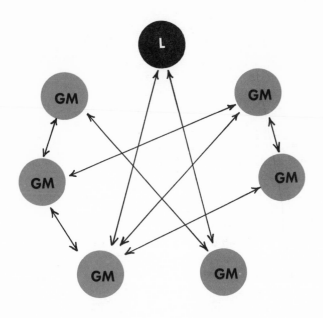

6. Suggests the purpose of the discussion.
7. Presents a tentative outline for the group to follow.
8. Requests the group members to react to the outline.
9. Requests group members to contribute to the topic to be discussed.
10. Keeps the discussion on the track, except when the majority of the group members indicate their desire to stray from the outline.
11. Strives to secure balanced participation from the group members.
12. Refrains from taking sides or making speeches.
13. Gives summaries when needed during the discussion and also at the close of the discussion.
14. Suggests further study or a course of action.
15. Evaluates the group's learning experience.

The Group Members

1. Assist in determining the topic to be discussed.
2. Read appropriate materials prior to the meeting.

3. Assist in defining the goals and procedures of the discussion.
4. Think intently about the topic to be discussed.
5. Listen actively to the contributions of the other group members.
6. Associate meanings with previous experiences.
7. Build upon the contributions of other group members.
8. Accept and support other group members as individuals of worth.
9. Help other group members to understand what is being said.
10. Strive for balanced participation of all group members.
11. Contribute only relevant information and opinions.
12. Identify new ideas and integrate these into their thinking.
13. Summarize the important areas of interest.
14. Determine how the information is to be used or what further study is to be made.
15. Assist in evaluating the group's learning experience.

Resources

Anderson, *Church Meetings that Matter*, entire book.
Bergevin, Morris, and Smith, *Adult Education Procedures*, pp. 95-106.
Day, *Dynamic Christian Fellowship*, entire book.
McKinley, *Creative Methods for Adult Classes*, pp. 55-67.

17. GROUP DRAWING

A group is divided into subgroups, each of which determines some common ideas about the assigned topic; these are then expressed through a drawing by one of the members of the subgroup. Later the drawings are shared with the entire group. In a very small group, the entire membership can work together on the project.

The Goal: To express ideas creatively through art.

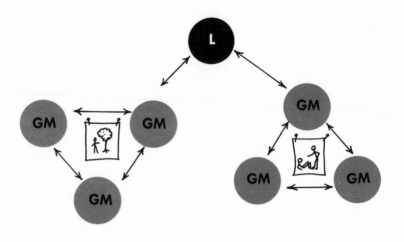

The Leader

1. Assists in determining a topic of interest.
2. Shows some pictures or reads some poems that assist in developing the topic.
3. Shows some examples of the possible kinds of contributions to be made.
4. Allows time for the group members to meditate on the topic.
5. Divides the group into subgroups of from three to four members each.
6. Requests the subgroup members to share common ideas about the topic.
7. Requests the subgroup members to determine how these ideas can be expressed through art.
8. Requests that one member of each subgroup express the ideas of that group in a picture or a series of pictures.
9. Requests the subgroups to share their ideas and the artistic representation of these with the members of the entire group.
10. Requests reactions from the group members to the ideas expressed through the art.
11. Summarizes the ideas that have been expressed through the art.
12. Suggests what this experience has meant to the lives of the group members and how it may benefit them.
13. Evaluates the group's learning experience.

The Group Members

1. Assist in determining a topic of interest.
2. Look at the pictures or listen to the poetry presented by the leader.
3. Think intently about the topic presented.
4. Contribute ideas about the topic.
5. Help to determine how these ideas can be expressed through art.
6. Assist the artist in each subgroup to express the ideas contributed by the group.
7. Share their contributions with the entire group.
8. Ask questions or make comments about the contributions of others.
9. Determine how this experience will affect their lives.
10. Assist in evaluating the group's learning experience.

18. GROUP RESPONSE TEAM

Several group representatives interrupt a speaker or resource person at appropriate times for immediate clarification of issues.

The Goal: To gain information and to clarify issues.

The Leader

1. Makes arrangements with the speaker prior to the meeting, and tells him what is expected of him.
2. Encourages the group members to do independent research prior to the meeting.
3. Prepares a podium for the speaker and a table and chairs for the group representatives and the leader.
4. Provides a signal system for the group representatives to use in notifying the speaker that they wish clarification of an issue.

32960

5. Selects three or four representatives from the group and informs them of their responsibilities.
6. Introduces the speaker and the group representatives to the group members.
7. Introduces the topic for discussion.
8. Acts as moderator of the meeting.
9. Suggests appropriate action or further study.
10. Evaluates the group's learning experience.

The Group Members

1. Read appropriate materials in preparation for the session.
2. Listen actively to what the speaker is saying.
3. Think intently about what is being said.
4. Associate meanings with previous experiences.
5. Identify new ideas and integrate these into their thinking.
6. Determine a course of action or a way of using information.
7. Assist in evaluating the group's learning experience.

The Group Representatives

1. Read appropriate materials in preparation for the session.
2. Listen intently to the speaker and other group representatives.
3. Be alert for issues that need clarification.
4. Signal the speaker when they desire clarification of an issue.

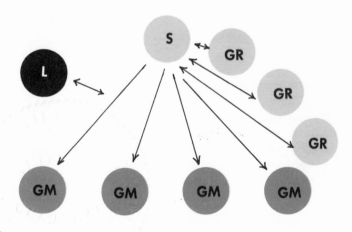

5. State concisely and explicitly the issues they wish clarified.
6. Assist in evaluating the group's learning experience.

The Speaker

1. Meets with the leader prior to the meeting.
2. Introduces the topic.
3. Presents the topic clearly, briefly, and informally.
4. Pauses to answer any questions that are asked by the group representatives.
5. Continues with his speech until interrupted again by one of the group representatives.
6. Summarizes the main issues of the topic.
7. Assists in evaluating his participation in the learning experience.

Resource

Bergevin, Morris, and Smith, *Adult Education Procedures*, pp. 188-190.

19. GROUP WRITING

A group is divided into subgroups, each of which determines some common ideas about an assigned topic; these are then expressed through a poem, litany, or other creative writing. Each subgroup works as a team in preparing their contributions which are later shared with other groups. In a very small group, the entire group can work together on the project.

The Goal: To express ideas through creative writing.

The Leader

1. Assists in determining a topic of interest.
2. Reads some poems, litanies, prose, or other creative writings to set the mood of the session.

3. Shows some examples of the possible kinds of contributions to be made.
4. Allows time for the group members to meditate on the topic.
5. Divides the group into subgroups of from three to four members each.
6. Requests the subgroup members to share common ideas about the topic.
7. Requests the subgroup members to determine how these ideas will be expressed through creative writing.
8. Requests that one member of each subgroup act as the recorder of that group's contributions.

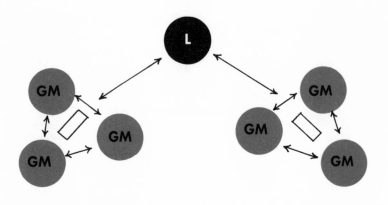

9. Requests the subgroups to share their ideas and creative writings with the entire group.
10. Requests reactions from the group members regarding the ideas expressed through the creative writing.
11. Summarizes the ideas that have been expressed.
12. Suggests what this experience may mean to the lives of the group members and how it may benefit them.
13. Evaluates the group's learning experience.

The Group Members

1. Assist in determining a topic of interest.
2. Listen intently to the creative writings read by the leader.

3. Think intensively about the topic presented.
4. Contribute ideas about the topic.
5. Help determine how these ideas can be expressed through creative writing.
6. Assist the group members to compose the creative writing.
7. Share their contributions with the entire group.
8. Inquire or comment about the contributions of others.
9. Determine how this experience will affect their lives.
10. Assist in evaluating the group's learning experience.

ALTERNATE SUGGESTION

The contributions of the subgroups can be arranged into a worship service experience.

20. INDUCTIVE BIBLE STUDY

A direct discovery of the meaning of a biblical passage is accomplished by discussing the questions, "What is the author saying?" "Why is the author saying it?" "When is the author saying it?" "Where is the author saying it?" "To whom is the author saying it?" "How is the author saying it?" Conclusions are drawn from these findings and an answer found to the question, "What does this mean to me?"

The Goal: To determine what the Bible passage means through a study of resources, and to determine how this will affect our lives.

The Leader

1. Provides resource books, such as Bibles, concordances, Bible dictionaries, Bible atlases, Bible commentaries.
2. Provides one or several tables on which these resource books are placed.
3. Prepares for each group written copies of the following questions relating to the Scripture passage to be studied:

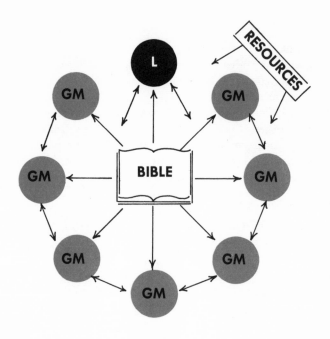

    a. What is the author saying?
    b. Why is the author saying it?
    c. When is the author saying it?
    d. Where is the author saying it?
    e. To whom is the author saying it?
    f. How is the author saying it?

4. Divides the group into subgroups or research teams to answer the questions with the aid of the resources available, and gives specific assignments to each subgroup.
5. Assists the group members if they need guidance in their study.
6. Requests reports from each research team.
7. Summarizes the material presented in the reports, or asks one of the group members to do so.
8. Suggests areas for further study or a course of action to follow.
9. Evaluates the group's learning experience.

The Group Members

1. Assist in determining the Bible passage to be studied.
2. Clarify what is expected of them.
3. Think intently about the tasks that are assigned to them.
4. Search for relevant information.
5. Read the materials carefully and record appropriate information.
6. Report relevant information to the other group members.
7. Identify new ideas and integrate these into their thinking.
8. Consider what this Scripture passage means to their lives.
9. Assist in evaluating the group's experiences.

Resources

Coiner, *Teaching the Word to Adults*, pp. 83-92.
LeBar, *Education that Is Christian*, pp. 154-156.

21. INTERVIEW FORUM

Opinions and facts are given spontaneously by an expert in response to questions from the leader; this is followed by free, open discussion among the entire group.

The Goal: To gain information from an expert about a specific topic and to respond to this information.

The Leader

1. Contacts the resource person who is to be interviewed and explains what is expected of him.
2. Encourages group members to do independent research prior to the meeting.
3. Introduces the resource person to the group members.
4. Introduces the topic to be discussed.
5. Asks questions of the resource person.

6. Requests questions from the group.
7. Summarizes the information presented.
8. Suggests a course of action or a way of using the information.
9. Evaluates the group's learning experience.

The Group Members

1. Read information in advance about the topic.
2. Listen actively to the contributions of the resource person and the leader.

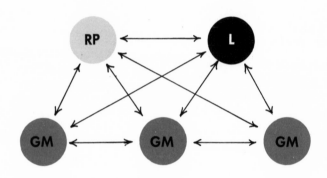

3. Think intently about the material presented.
4. Associate meanings with previous experiences.
5. Ask resource person questions that·are related to the topic.
6. Identify new ideas and integrate these into their thinking.
7. Determine a course of action to follow or a way to use the information gained.
8. Assist in evaluating the group's learning experience.

Resource Person

1. Meets with the leader prior to the meeting to determine what is expected of him.
2. Prepares relevant material about anticipated questions.
3. Answers any questions that are asked by the leader or the group members.
4. Summarizes the main issues presented.

5. Assists in evaluating the learning experience.

Resource

Bergevin, Morris, and Smith, *Adult Education Procedures*, pp. 106-116.

22. LECTURE

A prepared oral presentation is given by a qualified person.

The Goal: To gain information.

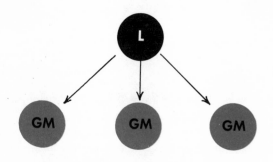

The Lecturer

1. Reads widely on the subject to be presented.
2. Selects relevant information.
3. Organizes the material into a meaningful outline.
4. Presents the material in a conversational manner.
5. Summarizes the main points of the presentation.
6. Suggests how this information can be used.
7. Evaluates the group's learning experience.

The Group Members

1. Read about the subject to be presented.
2. Listen actively to what the speaker is saying.
3. Think intently about the contributions of the speaker.
4. Associate meanings with previous experiences.
5. Take appropriate notes on the material presented.
6. Identify new ideas and integrate these into their thinking.
7. Determine how the information can be used.
8. Evaluate the group's learning experience.

Resources

Bergevin, Morris, and Smith, *Adult Education Procedures*, pp. 157-166.
Edge, *Helping the Teacher*, pp. 104-116.
Highet, *The Art of Teaching*, pp. 89-107.

23. LECTURE FORUM

A speech is followed immediately by active participation in a free, open discussion involving group members.

The Goal: To gain information and to clarify issues.

The Lecturer

1. Reads widely on the subject to be presented.
2. Selects relevant information.
3. Organizes the material into a meaningful outline.
4. Presents the material in a conversational manner.
5. Requests questions from the group members, who also respond to one another's reactions to the material presented.
6. Summarizes the main points of the presentation.
7. Suggests how the information can be used.
8. Evaluates the group's learning experience.

The Group Members

1. Read about the subject to be presented.
2. Listen actively to what the speaker is saying.
3. Think intently about the contributions which the speaker has made.
4. Associate meanings with previous experiences.
5. Take appropriate notes on the material presented.
6. Ask questions of the lecturer when requested.

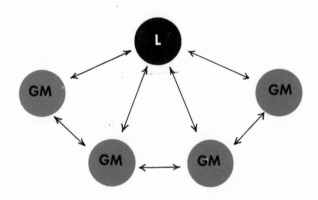

7. Respond to the ideas presented by the lecturer or by other group members during the preceding time of free and open discussion.
8. Identify new ideas and integrate them into their thinking.
9. Determine how the information is to be used.
10. Assist in evaluating the group's learning experience.

Note: In a large group, questions can be written on slips of paper, collected by ushers, and sorted by a moderator who then asks the questions of the lecturer.

Resource

Bergevin and Morris, *Group Processes for Adult Education*, pp. 17-19.

24. LISTENING TEAMS

A group is divided into several subgroups, each of which listens to something or somebody with a different question in mind. Later the ideas are shared with the entire group.

The Goal: To secure information or new ideas through participation that is directed to specific purposes.

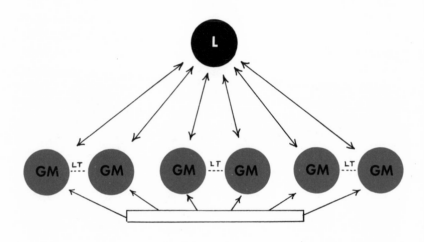

Listening Group 1   Listening Group 2   Listening Group 3

The Leader

1. Encourages the group members to do independent research prior to the meeting.
2. Introduces the topic.
3. Prior to a film, speech, or other presentation, divides the group into subgroups.
4. Presents each subgroup with specific questions to answer as they listen to the presentation.
5. After the presentation, requests reactions from the group members to the questions they were given.

6. Summarizes the contributions of the group, or requests someone else to do so.
9. Suggests a course of action or further study.
8. Evaluates the group's learning experience.

The Group Members

1. Read about the topic to be studied.
2. Consider the goals of the session.
3. Clarify instructions for the listening teams.
4. Listen actively to the presentation.
5. Associate meanings with previous experiences.
6. Contribute relevant information in response to the questions asked.
7. Identify new ideas and integrate these into their previous thinking.
8. Determine how the information can be used.
9. Assist in evaluating the group's learning experience.

Note: If desired, the listening teams may form buzz groups (see page 42) prior to sharing their reactions with all the members of the group.

Resources

Bergevin, Morris, and Smith, *Adult Education Procedures,* pp. 196-199.
Ford, *A Primer for Teachers and Leaders,* pp. 80-81.

25. MUSIC FORUM

A group listens to instrumental music and then responds to it by discussing the meanings of the moods and atmospheres that it creates. Or a group listens to choral music and follows this experience by discussing the meanings of the words and their significance to each individual.

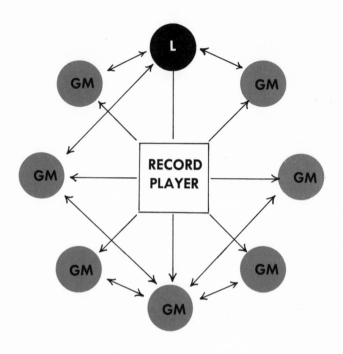

The Goal: To respond to music through group participation and discussion.

The Leader

1. Provides a record player which is placed in the center of the room. (If this is not possible, it is placed in the front of the room.)
2. Places chairs encircling the record player.
3. Introduces the purpose of the learning experience.
4. Suggests the items for which the group is to listen. (For example: How do you feel as you listen to the music? What mood does it create for you?) If desired, the leader may present a mimeographed list of moods that can be checked by the group members.
5. Plays the record.
6. Requests responses from the group members.
7. Plays portions of the record again, if appropriate.

84

8. Plays another record of contrasting mood.
9. Requests contributions from the group members about the contrasting moods of the two or more records.
10. Invites group members to indicate how they think these insights would apply to the use of music in the church.
11. Summarizes the insights gained from the discussion, or requests someone else to do it.
12. Suggests a course of action or a way to use the information.
13. Evaluates the group's learning experience.

The Group Members

1. Clarify the purpose of the session.
2. Understand how they are to listen.
3. Listen actively as the music is played.
4. Share ideas about the moods they felt while the music was being played.
5. React to one another's contributions.
6. Share ideas as to what this means to music in the church.
7. Determine a course of action or a way to use the information.
8. Assist in evaluating the group's learning experience.

26. PANEL

Several persons with specific knowledge informally discuss an assigned topic before a group.

The Goal: To gain information from a group of experts.

The Leader

1. Selects three or four group members prior to the session to serve as a panel, and informs them about the responsibilities they are to assume.
2. Prepares a list of questions he wishes the panel members to consider.

3. Meets with the panel members prior to the meeting to clarify issues and determine the procedure to follow.
4. Encourages the group members to do independent research prior to the meeting.
5. Places a table in the front of the room with the appropriate number of chairs for the panel members and himself.
6. Introduces the panel members to the group.
7. Introduces the topic for discussion.
8. Acts as moderator of the panel, asking questions of the panel members and securing participation from all of them, but not contributing his own ideas.
9. Clarifies issues as needed.
10. Summarizes the major contributions of the panel members.
11. Suggests a course of action or a way to use the information.
12. Evaluates the group's learning experience.

The Group Members

1. Read about the subject prior to the meeting.
2. Clarify the purpose of the session.
3. Listen actively to the panel members.

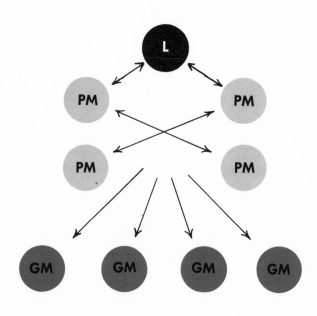

4. Think intently about the contributions of the panel members.
5. Take notes on appropriate materials.
6. Associate meanings with previous experiences.
7. Identify new ideas and integrate these into their thinking.
8. Determine a course of action or a way to use the information.
9. Assist in evaluating the group's learning experiences.

The Panel Members

1. Meet with the leader prior to the session to determine what is expected of them.
2. Read widely on the subject to be discussed.
3. Contribute to the discussion by reacting to the questions asked by the leader.
4. React to other panel members in appropriate ways.
5. Make sure that all panel members have an opportunity to react to questions.
6. Briefly summarize their contributions.
7. Assist in evaluating the group's learning experience.

Resources

Bergevin, Morris, and Smith, *Adult Education Procedures*, pp. 116-127.
McKinley, *Creative Methods for Adult Classes*, pp. 84-85.

27. PANEL FORUM

A panel discussion is followed immediately by free and open discussion among the entire group.

The Goal: To gain information from a group of experts, and to react to their contributions.

The Leader

1. Selects three or four group members prior to the session to serve as a panel and explains their responsibilities.

2. Prepares a list of questions he wishes the panel members to consider.
3. Meets with the panel members prior to the meeting to clarify issues and determine the procedure to follow.
4. Encourages the group members to do independent research prior to the meeting.
5. Places a table in the front of the room with the appropriate number of chairs for the panel members and himself.
6. Introduces the panel members to the group members.
7. Introduces the topic for discussion.
8. Acts as moderator of the panel, asking questions of the panel members and securing participation from all panel members, but not contributing his own ideas.
9. Clarifies issues as needed.
10. Requests group members to ask questions of the panel members and to make comments as desired.
11. Summarizes the major contributions of the participants.
12. Suggests a course of action or a way to use the information.
13. Evaluates the group's learning experience.

The Group Members

1. Read about the subject prior to the meeting.
2. Clarify the purpose of the session.
3. Listen actively to the panel members.
4. Think intently about the contributions of the panel members.
5. Take notes on appropriate materials, noting questions to ask the panel members when the leader requests such contributions.
6. Associate meanings with previous experiences.
7. Ask questions when the opportunity is given.
8. React to contributions of the panel members as well as of other group members.
9. Identify new ideas and integrate these into their thinking.
10. Determine a course of action or a way to use the information.
11. Assist in evaluating the group's learning experience.

The Panel Members

1. Meet with the leader prior to the meeting to determine what is expected of them.
2. Read widely on the subject to be discussed.

3. Contribute to the discussion by reacting to the questions asked by the leader.
4. React to the statements of other panel members in appropriate ways.
5. Make sure that all panel members have an opportunity to respond to questions.

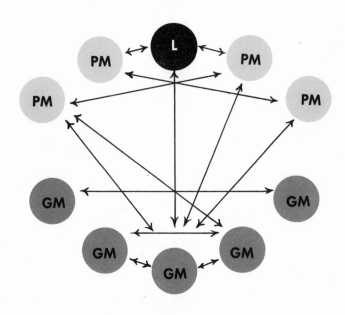

6. React to questions and comments which have been offered by the group members.
7. Briefly summarize their contributions.
8. Assist in evaluating the group's learning experience.

Resources

Bergevin and Morris, *Group Processes for Adult Education*, pp. 25-28.

Ford, *A Primer for Teachers and Leaders*, pp. 70-71.

28. PLAY-READING TALK-BACK

A play which presents a relevant problem is read to the group. Active audience participation in free, open discussion follows.

The Goal: To discuss a problem or issue.

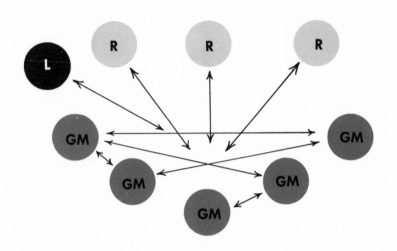

The Leader

1. Selects a play and the readers.
2. Rehearses the play-reading with the readers.
3. Prepares the room for the play-reading. (If the readers are to be seated, the leader provides high stools or a table and chairs; if the readers are to stand up, he provides music stands on which they can place their scripts.)
4. Introduces the play to the group members.
5. Suggests specific questions or items for which the group members are to listen. (Listening Teams may be used, if desired; see page 82.)
6. Requests comments from the group members regarding their reaction to the questions asked at the beginning of the play. (Buzz Groups may be used, if desired; see page 42.)

7. Summarizes the contributions of the group members.
8. Suggests a course of action or a way to use the information.
9. Evaluates the learning experience.

The Group Members

1. Clarify the purpose of the session.
2. Clarify what questions are to be answered while listening to the play-reading.
3. Listen actively to the play-reading.
4. Think intently about the words of the play.
5. Associate meanings with previous experiences.
6. Contribute reactions to the questions after the play is read.
7. Identify new ideas and integrate these into their thinking.
8. Determine a course of action or a way to use the information.
9. Assist in evaluating the group's learning experience.

The Play Readers

1. Read over the play to determine its meaning.
2. Identify themselves with the part(s) which they are to read.
3. Rehearse reading the play, using voice inflections that are appropriate to their roles.
4. Read the play before group members.
5. Contribute to the discussion of the play after it is read.
6. Assist in evaluating the learning experience.

Resources

Stirling, *Family Life Plays.*
Billups, *Discussion Starters for Youth Groups.*

29. QUESTIONS AND ANSWERS

Members of a group and the leader ask questions of each other. Or a group is presented with a list of questions on a given topic, from which they can ask those in which they have interest.

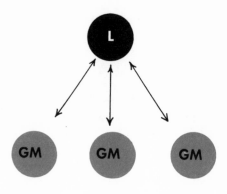

The Goal: To gain information and clarify issues.

The Leader

1. Encourages the group members to do independent research prior to the meeting.
2. Introduces a question-and-answer period on a given topic.
3. Asks questions of the group members.
4. Answers questions asked by the group members.
5. Summarizes the contributions of the session.
6. Suggests a course of action or a way to use the information.
7. Evaluates the learning experience.

The Group Members

1. Read about the topic before the session.
2. Answer questions asked by the leader.
3. Ask questions of the leader.
4. Determine a course of action or a way to use the information.
5. Assist in evaluating the group's learning experience.

ALTERNATE SUGGESTIONS

The Leader

1. Prepares a mimeographed list of questions on the topic.
2. Introduces the topic and presents the mimeographed sheets to the group members.
3. Requests group members to select the questions in which they have interest.

4. Answers the questions that the group members ask.
5. Summarizes the important issues considered.
6. Suggests a course of action or a way to use the information.
7. Evaluates the group's learning experience.

The Group Members

1. Read about the topic before the session.
2. Select the questions of interest to them and ask the leader for the answers.
3. Listen actively to the answers given.
4. Determine a course of action or a way to use the information.
5. Assist in evaluating the group's learning experience.

Resources

Bergevin, Morris, and Smith, *Adult Education Procedures*, pp. 199-203.
Caldwell, *Adults Learn and Like It*, pp. 64-69.
Edge, *Helping the Teacher*, pp. 76-85.

30. REACTION PANEL

Resource persons or representative members of a group hold a panel discussion before the group members, reacting to a speech, symposium, or film.

The Goal: To gain information and clarify issues.

The Leader

1. Selects the topic to be considered.
2. Encourages the group members to do independent research prior to the meeting.
3. Selects a speaker, symposium members, or a film.
4. Meets with the individuals to discuss the procedure of the meeting, or makes provision for the film to be available on the appropriate date.

5. Selects three or four group representatives or resource persons who are informed of their responsibilities and will act as panel members.
6. Provides a podium for the speaker, a table and chairs for the symposium members, or audiovisual equipment.
7. Provides a table and chairs for the panel members.
8. Introduces the topic to the group members and explains the procedure of the meeting.
9. Introduces the speaker, symposium members, or film to the group members.
10. Gives opportunity for the presentation of the speaker, symposium members, or film.
11. Acts as moderator of the panel as its members react to the speech or other presentation.
12. Summarizes the important issues presented.
13. Suggests a course of action or a way to use the information.
14. Evaluates the group's learning experience.

The Group Members

1. Read about the topic to be discussed, prior to the meeting.
2. Listen actively to the speaker, symposium members, or film.
3. Think intently about what is being said.
4. Associate meanings with previous experiences.
5. Identify new meanings and integrate these into their thinking.
6. Determine a course of action or a way to use the information.
7. Assist in evaluating the group's learning experience.

The Speaker (or Symposium Member)

1. Meets with the leader prior to the meeting to clarify his responsibilities and the procedure of the meeting.
2. Reads widely on the topic to be presented.
3. Prepares an outline of relevant information.
4. Delivers the speech in a conversational manner.
5. Joins the panel members as they react to the speech.
6. Assists in evaluating the learning experience.

The Reaction Panel Members

1. Meet with the leader prior to the meeting to clarify responsibilities.
2. Read widely on the topic to be presented.

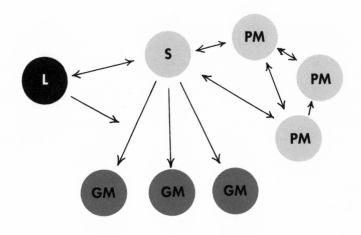

3. Listen actively to the speaker or other presentation.
4. Think intently as the speech is given and write down the issues they wish clarified after the speech is completed.
5. Ask questions or make comments on the speech in order to clarify issues or add an additional perspective.
6. Determine a course of action or a way to use the information.
7. Assist in evaluating the learning experience.

Resource

McKinley, *Creative Methods for Adult Classes*, pp. 92-93.

31. RESEARCH AND REPORT

A problem or issue is presented to the group. Research assignments are made and the researchers report their findings at a subsequent meeting (or at the close of the meeting).

The Goal: To gain information through research.

The Leader

1. Assists in selecting a problem or issue.
2. Leads the group in determining the needed areas of research on the topic.
3. Requests group members to volunteer to do research on the specific aspects determined by the group.
4. Suggests possible resources, or provides the resources, for the group members to use for the research.

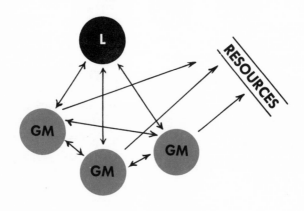

5. Asks for reports from the individuals at the subsequent meeting.
6. Requests reactions from other group members to the reports.
7. Summarizes the main points, or requests someone else to do this task.
8. Suggests a course of action or a way to use the information.
9. Evaluates the group's learning experience.

The Group Members

1. Assist in selecting a problem or issue facing them.
2. Assist the leader in determining the needed areas of research on the topic.
3. Volunteer to do research on specific areas.
4. Use the resources suggested by the leader and search for additional resources.

5. Study diligently on the specific assignment given.
6. Select relevant data.
7. Organize material to present to the group.
8. Report findings of their research.
9. Ask questions of other group members to clarify issues.
10. Determine a course of action or a way to use the information.
11. Assist in evaluating the group's learning experience.

ALTERNATE SUGGESTION

The research may be done in small groups during the class session and reports given at the close of the session.

32. ROLE-PLAYING

A problem situation is briefly acted out, with emphasis placed on individuals identifying with the characters. This is followed by a discussion of the problem presented. The following steps are necessary: Determine the exact circumstances of the problem situation; cast the players who in turn plan the method of presentation; act out the situation; stop the action at a climactic moment; analyze and discuss the role-play; and evaluate the results.

The Goal: To solve a problem and to have opportunity to enter into the feelings of others.

The Leader

1. Assists in selecting a problem or issues.
2. Determines and describes the exact circumstances of the situation to be role-played.
3. Determines the roles to be played and briefly describes them.
4. Requests volunteers to play the roles, suggesting that people volunteer for roles that are very different from their real life situations.

5. Requests role-players to leave the room for a brief time (from two to three minutes) to discuss the procedure of their role-play.
6. While role-players are preparing for their participation, gives more information to the remaining group members regarding the problem to be role-played.
7. Calls time for the players to return to the room to give their presentation.
8. Cuts off the action of the role-play at a climactic moment.
9. Instructs the role-players to discontinue their roles.
10. Requests the group members to analyze and discuss the role-play, possible solutions, and its implications for them.
11. Requests the role-players to report on how they felt in the roles that they played.
12. Summarizes the main issues in solving the problem.
13. Suggests a course of action or a way to use the information.
14. Evaluates the learning experience.

The Group Members

1. Assist in selecting a problem or issue facing them.
2. Suggest the exact circumstances of the situation to be role-played.
3. Listen actively to the leader as he explains the details of the role-playing situation.
4. Listen actively to the role-playing situation.
5. Think intently about the problem to be solved.
6. Share reactions to the role-playing situation and suggest solutions.
7. Determine a course of action or a way to use the information which has been gained.
8. Assist in evaluating the group's learning experience.

The Role-Players (Group Representatives)

1. Volunteer for parts in the role-playing situation, each selecting a role that is very different from the one which he plays in real life.
2. Identify themselves with the role of another person, each trying to feel what the other person would feel in the specific situation.
3. Determine the sequence of actions.

4. Act out the situation.
5. Stop action when leader calls time.
6. Resume their normal life-roles.
7. Respond to the feelings they had while playing the role of another person.
8. React to the reasons for the behavior of the individuals in the role-play.
9. Determine what this situation means to them.
10. Assist in evaluating the learning experience.

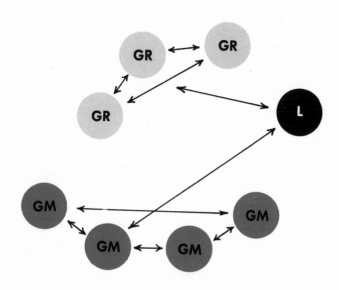

Resources

Bergevin, Morris, and Smith, *Adult Education Procedures*, pp. 135-147.
How to Use Role Playing, entire book.
Klein, *Role Playing in Leadership Training and Group Problem Solving*, entire book.
Strauss, *New Ways to Better Meetings*, pp. 91-110.

33. SCREENED SPEECH

The group is divided into subgroups which select special areas of concern. They present these to the speaker, who addresses himself to their questions through a speech.

The Goal: To gain information according to the interest of a group.

The Leader

1. Selects a topic to be considered.
2. Contacts a speaker and gives him information regarding the procedure of the meeting.
3. Introduces the topic to the group members and suggests possible areas of concern related to the topic.
4. Divides the group into subgroups of from three to six persons each.
5. Suggests that each subgroup list some questions related to the topic on which they would like the speaker to comment. (See Buzz Groups, page 42, for specific instructions.)
6. Calls the group to reassemble.
7. Collects the slips of paper on which questions are recorded and quickly sorts them into general areas of interest. (If desired, the recorders from each buzz group may be requested to respond directly to the speaker.)
8. Reports to the speaker about the areas of concern that the group members have listed regarding the topic, and requests the speaker to react to these in the speech.
9. Summarizes the main points of interest after the speech.
10. Suggests a course of action or a way of using the information.
11. Evaluates the group's learning experience.

The Group Members

1. Clarify the topic to be discussed.
2. Select specific areas of interest within the topic to be suggested to the speaker for comment.
3. Record the areas of interest on slips of paper.
4. Listen actively to what the speaker is saying.
5. Think intently about the topic.
6. Associate meanings with previous experiences.
7. Identify new ideas and integrate these into their thinking.

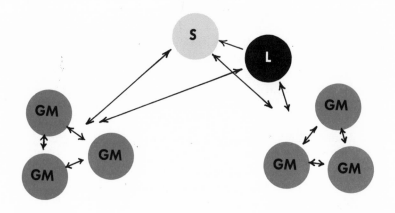

8. Determine a course of action or a way of using the information.
9. Assist in evaluating the group's learning experience.

The Speaker

1. Meets with the leader prior to the meeting to determine the procedure of the meeting.
2. Reads widely on the topic to be presented.
3. Considers a broad range of knowledge regarding the topic. (He may wish to prepare a mimeographed list of specific areas of interest which will be offered to the group members for selection.)
4. Listens carefully when the leader presents the areas of concern selected by the group members.
5. Notes these areas of concern on a piece of paper.
6. Quickly organizes the areas of concern into an outline and presents his speech as an answer to the questions asked by the group members.
7. Assists in evaluating the learning experience.

Resources

Bergevin, Morris, and Smith, *Adult Education Procedures*, pp. 203-206.
McKinley, *Creative Methods for Adult Classes*, pp. 93-94.

34. SEMINAR

A group of persons convenes for research study under the leadership of an expert.

The Goal: To gain information through study and discussion.

The Leader

1. Guides the selection of a pertinent problem or issue which the group is to study.
2. Requests reports from group members on areas of research.
3. Asks for reactions from other group members regarding the reports.
4. Summarizes the main points of the research reports.
5. Suggests a course of action or a way of using the information.
6. Evaluates the group's learning experience.

The Group Members

1. Select an area of interest or concern on which they desire to do research.
2. Do research on the area of interest selected.
3. Present the research to the other group members.
4. React to the presentations of other group members.
5. Determine a course of action or a way of using the information.
6. Assist in evaluating the group's learning experience.

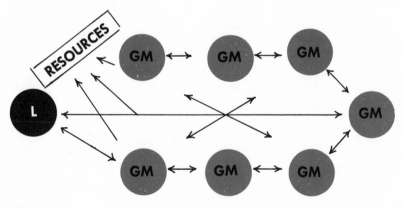

Resources

Bergevin, Morris, and Smith, *Adult Education Procedures,* pp. 147-156.

McKinley, *Creative Methods for Adult Classes,* pp. 68-75.

35. SERMON FORUM

A sermon is followed by discussion in small groups. These small groups then join together for further discussion of the topic.

The Goal: To respond to a pastor's sermon in order to clarify issues and expand knowledge.

The Pastor

STEP 1

1. Selects a topic and prepares his sermon. (He may prepare a mimeographed outline of the sermon or a list of questions to be considered.)
2. Delivers the sermon.
3. Introduces the leader or moderator of the forum.

STEP 2

4. Visits with the moderator or leader as the subgroups meet.

STEP 3

5. Answers questions asked by group members.
6. Summarizes the main issues.
7. Evaluates the group's learning experience.

The Moderator or Leader of the Forum

STEP 1

1. Meets with the pastor prior to the meeting to plan all details: the order of activities, the places of meeting of the subgroups, and the equipment needed.
2. Prepare the room(s) for the subgroups.

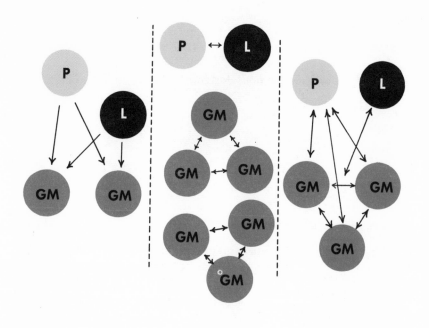

STEP 1   STEP 2   STEP 3

3. After he is introduced by the pastor, requests the group members to react to the sermon.

4. Divides the group into subgroups and designates where they are to meet.

5. Gives the subgroups instructions about their responsibilities. (Gives them a list of questions if these are available.)

6. Requests each subgroup to prepare a list of questions related to the sermon for the pastor to answer.

7. Instructs the subgroups concerning the time limit for their task.

STEP 2

8. Visits with the pastor as the subgroups meet.

9. Gives a warning time of two minutes for the subgroups.

10. Requests the subgroups to reassemble into one group.

STEP 3

11. Requests the subgroups to present their questions or comments on the sermon.

12. Directs the questions to the pastor.
13. Suggests a course of action or a way of using the information, after the pastor has summarized the main issues.
14. Assists in evaluating the learning experience.

The Group Members

STEP 1

1. Listen actively to the sermon.
2. Think intently about what is being said by the pastor.
3. Associate meaning with previous experiences.
4. Take notes on items of interest and areas to be clarified.

STEP 2

5. Share with other members of the subgroups the items which they wish clarified, areas to be challenged, or comments to be made.
6. List specific questions to be asked of the pastor.

STEP 3

7. Share areas of concern that need clarification.
8. Express ideas that either reinforce or challenge the pastor's statements.
9. Determine a course of action or a way to use the information.
10. Assist in evaluating the group's learning experience.

Resources

McKinley, *Creative Methods for Adult Classes*, pp. 47-54.
Thompson, *A Listener's Guide to Preaching*.

36. SYMPOSIUM

A series of speeches is given by as many speakers as there are aspects of a problem or issue.

The Goal: To gain information from a group of experts.

The Leader

1. Selects an issue or problem facing the group.
2. Determines various aspects of this issue or problem.
3. Encourages the group members to do independent research prior to the meeting.
4. Selects as many experts as there are aspects of the issue, requesting each expert to deal with one aspect.
5. Requests each expert to prepare a brief speech on the aspect of the issue which has been designated to him.

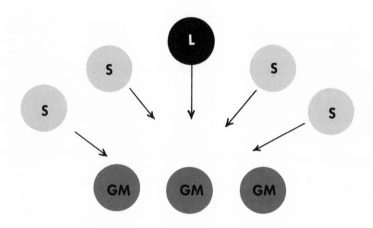

6. Meets with the symposium members (speakers) prior to the meeting to determine the procedure to be followed.
7. Places a table in the front of the room with the appropriate number of chairs for the experts and himself.
8. Introduces the speakers to the group members.
9. Introduces the topic to be presented.
10. Introduces each aspect of the topic in turn and requests the appropriate expert to speak to it.
11. Summarizes the major contributions of the experts.
12. Suggests a course of action, areas of further study, or a way to use the information.
13. Evaluates the group's learning experience.

The Group Members

1. Read about the subject prior to the meeting.
2. Listen actively to the speakers.
3. Think intently about the contributions of the speakers.
4. Take notes on appropriate materials.
5. Associate meanings with previous experiences.
6. Identify new ideas and integrate these into their thinking.
7. Determine a course of action, areas of further study, or a way to use the information.
8. Assist in evaluating the group's learning experience.

The Speakers

1. Meet with the leader prior to the meeting to determine what is expected of them.
2. Read widely on the subject to be presented, and specifically on the aspect of the issue that is assigned to them.
3. Prepare a brief speech on the aspect of the issue assigned to them.
4. Present the speeches to the group members.
5. Assist in evaluating the learning experience.

Resources

Bergevin, Morris, and Smith, *Adult Education Procedures,* pp. 175-186.
Ford, *A Primer for Teachers and Leaders,* pp. 86-87.
McKinley, *Creative Methods for Adult Classes,* pp. 85-87.

37. SYMPOSIUM DIALOGUE

An expert or resource person reacts to a series of speeches given by as many speakers as there are aspects of a problem or issue.

The Goal: To gain information from a group of experts.

The Leader

1. Selects an issue or problem facing the group.
2. Determines various aspects of this issue or problem.
3. Encourages the group members to do independent research prior to the meeting.
4. Selects as many speakers as there are aspects of the issue or problem, requesting each speaker to deal with one aspect of this.
5. Requests each speaker to prepare a brief speech on the aspect of the issue or problem which has been designated to him.
6. Selects an expert (resource person) who understands all of the aspects of the problem.
7. Requests the expert to react to the speakers' contributions.
8. Meets with the expert and speakers prior to the meeting to determine the procedure to follow.
9. Places two tables in the front of the room: one for the speakers and the other for the expert (resource person) and himself.
10. Introduces the participants to the group members and explains the procedure of the meeting.
11. Outlines the topic to be presented.
12. Introduces each aspect of the topic in turn and requests the appropriate speaker to speak to it.
13. Requests the expert to react to the speeches.
14. Summarizes the major contributions of the participants.
15. Suggests a course of action, further study, or a way to use the information.
16. Evaluates the group's learning experience.

The Group Members

1. Read about the subject prior to the meeting.
2. Listen actively to the speakers.
3. Think intently about the contributions of the speakers.
4. Take notes on appropriate materials.
5. Associate meanings with previous experiences.
6. Identify new ideas and integrate these into their thinking.
7. Determine a course of action, areas of further study, or a way to use the information.
8. Assist in evaluating the group's learning experience.

The Speakers

1. Meet with the leader prior to the meeting to determine what is expected of them.
2. Read widely on the subject to be presented, and specifically on the aspect of the issue that is assigned to them.
3. Prepare a brief speech on the aspect of the issue assigned to them.
4. Present the speeches to the group members.
5. Listen actively to the reactions of the expert to their presentations.
6. Assist in evaluating the learning experience.

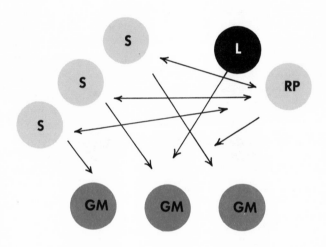

The Expert (Resource Person)

1. Meets with the leader and the speakers prior to the meeting to determine the procedure to be followed.
2. Reads widely on the subject to be presented.
3. Reacts to the speeches, presenting both support and challenge.
4. Adds additional information that is significant.
5. Assists in evaluating the learning experience.

38. SYMPOSIUM FORUM

A symposium is held, followed by informal discussion by the entire group.

The Goal: To gain information from a group of experts and to have opportunity to clarify the issues.

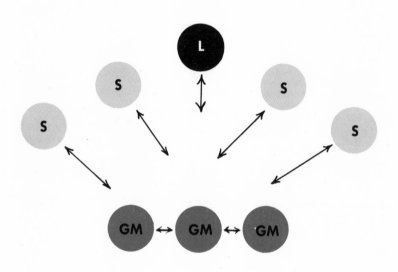

The Leader

1. Selects an issue or problem.
2. Determines various aspects of this issue or problem.
3. Selects as many experts (speakers) as there are aspects of the issue, requesting each to deal with one aspect.
4. Requests each expert to prepare a brief speech on the aspect which has been assigned to him.
5. Meets with the symposium members (speakers) prior to the meeting to determine the procedure to be followed.
6. Encourages the group members to do independent research prior to the meeting.

7. Places a table and chairs in the front of the room.
8. Introduces the speakers to the group members.
9. Introduces the topic to be presented.
10. Introduces each aspect of the topic in turn, and requests the appropriate expert to speak to it.
11. Requests the group members to react to the speeches by asking questions or giving additional information.
12. Summarizes the major contributions of the meeting.
13. Suggests a course of action, areas of further study, or a way to use the information.
14. Evaluates the group's learning experience.

The Group Members

1. Read about the subject prior to the meeting.
2. Listen actively to the speakers.
3. Think intently about the contributions of the speakers.
4. Take notes on appropriate materials and on areas that need clarification.
5. Associate meanings with previous experiences.
6. React to the speakers when the opportunity is given by asking questions or giving additional information.
7. Identify new ideas and integrate these into their thinking.
8. Determine a course of action, areas of further study, or a way to use the information.
9. Assist in evaluating the group's learning experience.

The Speakers (Experts)

1. Meet with the leader prior to the meeting to determine what is expected of them.
2. Read widely on the subject to be presented, and specifically on the aspect of the issue that is assigned to them.
3. Prepare a brief speech on the aspect assigned to them.
4. Present the speeches to the group members.
5. Answer the questions asked by the group members.
6. Assist in evaluating the group's learning experience.

Resources

Bergevin and Morris, *Group Processes for Adult Education*, pp. 33-36.
Ford, *A Primer for Teachers and Leaders*, pp. 88-89.

39. WORK GROUPS

A group is divided into subgroups to accomplish a given task or tasks.

The Goal: To accomplish a task or tasks through working together as a group.

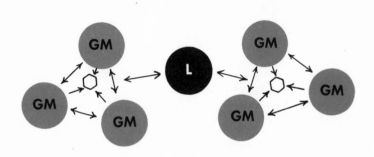

The Leader

1. Assists in determining the problem or issue.
2. Assists in determining the areas of concern connected with the problem or issue which can help the group to understand it better or to perform some function related to it.
3. Determines specific tasks to be performed. (The same task may be performed by several subgroups or by all subgroups, or each subgroup may have a different task to perform.)
4. Divides the group into subgroups and provides resource materials when needed.
5. Gives instructions to the subgroups regarding the accomplishment of their tasks.
6. Rotates among the subgroups to determine which ones need assistance.
7. Calls time for subgroups to reassemble, unless the activity extends over a long period of time or is performed outside of the session.
8. Requests subgroups to report on the accomplishments achieved.

9. Requests reactions to the accomplishments of the tasks.
10. Suggests a course of action, further research, or a way to use the experience as a basis for future action.
11. Evaluates the learning experience.

The Group Members

1. Assist in determining a problem or issue of interest.
2. Assist in determining specific tasks to be performed that are related to the problem or issue.
3. Listen actively to the instructions given for the work-group projects.
4. Become actively involved in performing the task assigned to them or chosen by them, using the available resources.
5. Report findings of the accomplished task.
6. Share their responses to the findings of other subgroups.
7. Determine how this experience can be used as a basis for future action.
8. Assist in evaluating the learning experience.

Resource

Little, *Learning Together in the Christian Fellowship,* pp. 39-40.

40. WORKSHOP

A group of persons with a common interest gather together, under the leadership of several experts, to explore one or more specific aspects of a topic. Subgroups are formed for the purpose of hearing speeches, seeing demonstrations, discussing various aspects of the topic, studying, working, practicing, and evaluating.

The Goal: To gain information through experience and sharing information.

The Leader

1. Assists in determining a problem or issue facing the group.

113

2. Aids in discovering various areas of interest related to this issue or problem.
3. Selects and contacts resource persons for each area of interest to be explored.
4. Meets with all the resource persons prior to the session to determine what is expected of them.
5. Provides rooms, equipment, and resource materials according to the needs of the resource persons.
6. Encourages the group members to do independent research prior to the meeting.

STEP 1

7. Assembles the entire group and informs them of the purpose of the workshop and the various aspects of the topic to be considered.
8. Asks each of the group members to select an area of interest or need that they wish to explore.
9. Introduces the resource persons who will deal with each aspect of the topic.
10. Gives instructions regarding the rooms where the individual interest groups will meet.

STEP 2

11. Makes himself available to resource persons and group members.
12. Evaluates the learning experience.

The Group Members

1. Assist in determining an area of interest.
2. Assist in determining subtopics of this area of interest.
3. Read about the topic prior to the meeting.

STEP 1

4. Listen actively to the introduction of the topic and the areas of concern related to it.
5. Determine the areas of interest and need which they would like to explore.
6. Select the group in which they would like to participate.

STEP 2

7. Listen actively to the resource person.
8. Participate in the activity provided in each subgroup.

114

9. Associate meanings with previous experience.
10. Identify new ideas and integrate these into their thinking.
11. Determine how this experience can be used to benefit them.
12. Assist in evaluating the learning experience.

The Resource Persons

1. Meet with the leader in order to determine responsibilities.
2. Read widely on the topic assigned.
3. Secure necessary resources and equipment or make requests known to the leader.

STEP 1

4. Briefly introduce the area of interest to the entire group.

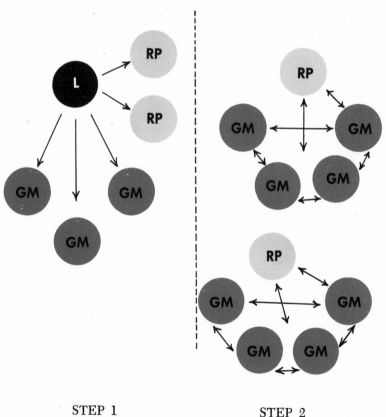

STEP 1   STEP 2

5. Present introductory material to the group members who have selected their specialized area of study.
6. Arrange for demonstrations, work groups, discussions, or other means of participation by the group members.
7. Assist group members in their participation.
8. Request reports or results of the work projects of individuals or groups.
9. Summarize the activities of their work groups.
10. Suggest areas of action or how the information can be used.
11. Assist in evaluating the learning experience.

Resources

Beckhard, *How to Plan and Conduct Workshops and Conferences,* entire book.

Bergevin, Morris, and Smith, *Adult Education Procedures,* pp. 224-225, 229-230.

4.
evaluation

WHY EVALUATE?

Evaluation gives direction to a learning situation. How will you know whether you have achieved your goals unless you evaluate your accomplishments? Evaluation also assists you as a teacher or leader in determining future learning experiences; it helps you to know whether you are challenging the students to study and learn. Evaluation produces an alert attitude on the part of the teacher and the learner; it allows the leader to know if the amount of instruction, the kinds of ways used to motivate learning, and the rate at which learning is taking place are effective. It gives the learner a sense of accomplishment or a clue to where he fell short.

WHEN TO EVALUATE?

The leader and the group members should be constantly evaluating their learning experiences. Before the session, the leader should plan for specific ways of evaluating the session for the day. During the session, the leader and the group members should be alert to the happenings to determine whether real and effective learning is taking place. After the session, the leader and the group members should take time to determine what experiences have been effective and what experiences could have been improved.

WHO SHOULD EVALUATE?

Everyone who is involved in the learning experience should have an opportunity to participate in evaluation. Each person, whether leader, resource person, or group member, has a different perspective on the learning situation. Without participation by all, evaluation cannot be valid.

WHAT TO EVALUATE?

Since evaluation provides an opportunity to determine whether goals are achieved, and since the goals set are stated in terms of changes that are sought in the learners, evaluation must determine what, if any, changes have taken place.

The desired changes are in the areas of *knowing, feeling,* and *doing* (see pages 25-27). It is easier to measure changes in things known than to determine changes in feeling and doing, but the latter are just as necessary as the former. Some indication of changes in feeling can be given by questionnaires on which group members check what kinds of attitude-changes they think have taken place. Changes in action can be evidenced by the overt behavior of individuals.

HOW TO EVALUATE?

The most widely used means of evaluation is a post-reaction sheet which gives the group members opportunity to express their opinions of the learning situation at the end of the session. Three very simple questions can be asked: What did you like best? What did you like least? What was most helpful to you? In some instances, it would be more desirable to prepare a list of questions where the group members can check their responses.

The following lists of questions present some suggestions from which you can compile your own post-reaction sheets.

General questions

1. What did you like best about the session?
2. What did you like least about the session?
3. What will be most useful to you?
4. What did you learn from the session today?
5. What specific things came up today that you would have liked to explore further?

6. How would you suggest the session could have been improved?

Contrasting statements

Instructions: Circle one of the five points on the scale which most nearly represents your reaction in relation to the contrasting statement at each end of the scale.

1. How did you like the session today?
   Excellent   5   4   3   2   1   Poor

2. Were the purposes clear?
   Very clear   5   4   3   2   1   Not clear

3. How well did the group work together?
   Very well   5   4   3   2   1   Poorly

4. How did you feel as a member of the group?
   Accepted   5   4   3   2   1   Rejected

5. How did you feel that the subject matter was presented?
   Very well   5   4   3   2   1   Poorly

6. How did you feel about participating in the discussion?
   Very free   5   4   3   2   1   Very inhibited

7. How interested were you in the topic?
   Very interested   5   4   3   2   1   Not at all interested

8. Did you gain any new ideas or insights about the problem?
   Many   5   4   3   2   1   None

9. How suitable was the method of teaching?
   Very suitable   5   4   3   2   1   Not at all suitable

10. How relaxed did you feel?
    Completely
    relaxed   5   4   3   2   1   Extremely tense

Open-ended questions [1]

Reactions to what happened in the session:

1. The most helpful thing that happened to me today was _____

_____.

[1] Some questions adapted from *Sample Group Evaluation Forms* (Washington: National Training Laboratories, 1958).

2. Today it would have been helpful if someone _____
_____.

3. Considering the things that people did today, I tended to admire _____.

_____.

4. Our progress was hindered today when _____

5. I was somewhat surprised at _____

6. It was disappointing when _____

7. It was encouraging to me when _____

8. I felt uncomfortable when _____

9. I had a comfortable feeling when _____

10. I had a feeling of disapproval when _____

11. I had a feeling of approval when _____

_____.

Frequently we think of evaluation as the end of the learning experience, but it should be the *beginning* of progress. Evaluation is of value only if you use it to improve yourself and your manner of assisting others to learn effectively.

bibliography

Anderson, Philip A., *Church Meetings that Matter.* Philadelphia: United Church Press, 1965, 112 pp.

Atkinson, C. Harry, *Building and Equipping for Christian Education.* New York: National Council of Churches of Christ in the U.S.A., revised edition, 1963, 87 pp.

Beckhard, Richard, *How to Plan and Conduct Workshops and Conferences.* New York: Association Press, 1956, 64 pp.

Bergevin, Paul, and Morris, Dwight, *Group Processes for Adult Education.* New York: The Seabury Press, revised edition, 1955, 86 pp.

————————, *A Manual for Group Discussion Participants.* New York: The Seabury Press, 1965, 73 pp.

Bergevin, Paul, Morris, Dwight, and Smith, Robert M., *Adult Education Procedures.* New York: The Seabury Press, 1963, 245 pp.

Billups, Ann, *Discussion Starters for Youth Groups.* Valley Forge: The Judson Press, 1966, 224 pp.

Caldwell, Irene, *Adults Learn and Like It.* Anderson: The Warner Press, 1955, 112 pp.

————————, *Teaching that Makes a Difference.* Anderson: The Warner Press, Revised edition, 1962, 95 pp.

Clark, Charles Hutchison, *Brainstorming.* New York: Doubleday, 1958, 262 pp.

Clemmons, Robert S., *Dynamics of Christian Adult Education.* Nashville: Abingdon Press, 1958, 143 pp.

Coiner, Harry G., *Teaching the Word to Adults.* St. Louis: Concordia Publishing House, 1962, 129 pp.

Day, LeRoy J., *Dynamic Christian Fellowship.* Valley Forge: The Judson Press, 1960, 101 pp.

Dialogue with the World: Church Group Discussion Handbook for Theatrical Films. New York: Encyclopedia Britannica Films, Inc., 1964, 68 pp.

Edge, Findley B., *Helping the Teacher.* Nashville: Broadman Press, 1959, 181 pp.

——————, *Teaching for Results.* Nashville: Broadman Press, 1956, 230 pp.

Fallaw, Wesner, *The Case Method in Pastoral and Lay Education.* Philadelphia: Westminster Press, 1963, 207 pp.

Ford, LeRoy, *A Primer for Teachers and Leaders.* Nashville: Broadman Press, 1963. 141 pp.

Group Leadership. Valley Forge: Division of Christian Education, American Baptist Convention, 1962, 14 pp.

Highet, Gilbert, *The Art of Teaching.* New York: Vintage Books, 1954, 259 pp.

How to Use Role Playing. Washington, D.C.: Adult Education Association of the U.S.A., 1955, 48 pp.

How to Teach Adults. Washington, D.C.: Adult Education Association of the U.S.A., 1955, 48 pp.

Howe, Reuel L., *The Miracle of Dialogue.* New York: The Seabury Press, 1963, 154 pp.

Kidd, James R., *How Adults Learn.* New York: Association Press, 1959, 324 pp.

Klein, Alan F., *Role Playing in Leadership Training and Group Problem Solving.* New York: Association Press, 1956, 176 pp.

Klein, Wilma H., LeShan, Eda J., and Furman, Sylvan S., *Promoting Mental Health of Older People through Group Methods.* New York: Mental Health Materials Center, 1965, 156 pp.

Koenig, Robert E., *The Use of the Bible with Adults.* Philadelphia: United Church Press, 1959, 183 pp.

Kuhn, Margaret E., *You Can't Be Human Alone.* New York: National Council of Churches, 1956, 55 pp.

LeBar, Lois E., *Education that is Christian.* Westwood, New Jersey: Fleming H. Revell Co., 1958, 252 pp.

Little, Sara, *Learning Together in the Christian Fellowship.* Richmond: John Knox Press, 1956, 104 pp.

Liveright, A. A., *Strategies of Leadership in Conducting Adult Education Programs.* New York: Harper & Row, Publishers, Inc., 1959, 140 pp.

McBurney, James H. and Mills, Glen E., *Argumentation and Debate.* New York: Macmillan Company, Second edition, 1964, 474 pp.

McKinley, John, *Creative Methods for Adult Classes.* St. Louis, Missouri: The Bethany Press, 1960, 96 pp.

McKinley, John and Smith, Robert M., *Guide to Program Planning: A Handbook.* New York: The Seabury Press, 1965, 29 pp.

Miller, Harry L., *Teaching and Learning in Adult Education.* New York: Macmillan Company, 1964, 340 pp.

Miller, Randolph Crump, *Education for Christian Living.* Englewood Cliffs, New Jersey: Prentice-Hall, Inc., Second edition, 1963, 462 pp.

Morgan, Barton, and others, *Methods in Adult Education*. Danville, Illinois: Interstate Printers and Publishers, Inc., 1960, 180 pp.

Planning and Leading Large Meetings (An adult leadership leaflet). Philadelphia: Department of Adult Program, The United Presbyterian Church in the U.S.A., 15 pp.

Rohrbough, John and Getsinger, J. Wilson, "Chain Reaction Forum," in *Adult Leadership*, vol. 6, no. 5, Nov. 1957, pp. 131, 140.

Snyder, Alton G., *Teaching Adults*. Valley Forge, Pa.: The Judson Press, 1959, 93 pp.

Snyder, Ross, *Depth and Encounter Study of the Bible*. Valley Forge: Department of Ministry with Youth, American Baptist Convention, 1960, 8 pp.

Stirling, Nora, *Family Life Plays*. New York: Association Press, 1961.

Strauss, Bert and Frances, *New Ways to Better Meetings*. New York: The Viking Press, Inc., Revised edition, 1964, 177 pp.

Thelen, Herbert A., *Dynamics of Groups at Work*. Chicago: The University of Chicago Press, 1954, Paperback, 1963, 379 pp.

Thompson, William D., *A Listener's Guide to Preaching*. Nashville: Abingdon Press, 1966, 110 pp.

Warren, Virginia (ed.), *A Treasury of Techniques for Teaching Adults*. Washington, D.C.: National Association for Public School Adult Education, 1964, 48 pp.

appendix

A SAMPLE LESSON PLAN

Getting Ready

Determine:

1. The goal(s) to be achieved
2. The main questions to be asked
3. Available resources
4. Ways to achieve the goals
5. Method of evaluation
6. Physical arrangements that need attention

   Temperature of the room
   Lighting
   Ventilation
   Place of chairs, tables, podium, chalkboard, newsprint,
     and other equipment
   Name tags, if the persons are not acquainted

Outlining the Procedure

Introduction
Development of the learning experiences
Conclusion or Summary
Evaluation

32960